T0295844

# Collaborative Governance of Local Governments in China

China faces the problem of collaboration deficiency in local governance of metropolitan areas. With the evolution of regional spatial structure in China, this book is timely with its analysis on how China can approach current problems in China's regional governance through a holistic collaborative governance mechanism.

The book applies the governance theory to the local government in metropolitan areas and explains how this approach may help to equalize regional public resources allocation. The author puts forth a convincing case for the use of holistic collaborative governance to better understand the problems of China's local government in metropolitan areas and to promote regional government collaboration. The book also looks at cross-jurisdiction collaboration organization, collaborative mechanism of local government, private sector and non-governmental organizations in public affairs (environmental protection, transportation, public health, water resources).

**Jing Cui** is Professor of Public Administration at the School of Government in Central University of Finance and Economics, China.

## Routledge Focus on Public Governance in Asia

Series Editors:

Hong Liu

*Nanyang Technological University, Singapore*

Wenxuan Yu

*Xiamen University, China*

Focusing on new governance challenges, practices and experiences in and about a globalizing Asia, particularly East Asia and Southeast Asia, this focus series invites upcoming and established researchers all over the world to succinctly and comprehensively discuss important public administration and policy themes such as government administrative reform, public budgeting reform, government crisis management, public private partnership, science and technology policy, technology-enabled public service delivery, public health and aging, talent management, and anticorruption across Asian countries. The book series presents compact and concise content under 50,000 words long which have significant theoretical contributions to the governance theory with an Asian perspective and practical implications for administration and policy reform and innovation.

**The Two Sides of Korean Administrative Culture**
Competitiveness or Collectivism?
*Tobin Im*

**Political Economic Perspectives of China's Belt and Road Initiative**
Reshaping Regional Integration
*Christian Ploberger*

**Exploring Public-Private Partnerships in Singapore**
The Success-Failure Continuum
*Soojin Kim and Kai Xiang Kwa*

**Collaborative Governance of Local Governments in China**
*Jing Cui*

For more information about this series, please visit www.routledge.com/Routledge-Focus-on-Public-Governance-in-Asia/book-series/RFPGA

# Collaborative Governance of Local Governments in China

Jing Cui

LONDON AND NEW YORK

First published 2020
by Routledge
2 Park Square, Milton Park, Abingdon, Oxon OX14 4RN

and by Routledge
52 Vanderbilt Avenue, New York, NY 10017

*Routledge is an imprint of the Taylor & Francis Group, an informa business*

© 2020 Jing Cui

*British Library Cataloguing-in-Publication Data*
A catalogue record for this book is available from the British Library

*Library of Congress Cataloging-in-Publication Data*
A catalog record has been requested for this book

ISBN: 978-0-367-15008-2 (hbk)
ISBN: 978-0-429-05445-7 (ebk)

Typeset in Times New Roman
by Wearset Ltd, Boldon, Tyne and Wear

# Contents

# Figures

# Tables

# Acknowledgments

This book is an outcome of my accumulated efforts during the past several years. I am deeply indebted to my colleagues and friends who have kindly offered advice and assistance over the years in writing and revising the manuscript. I received immeasurable support from the Central University of Finance and Economics, which provides the financial support for me in the project of "Longma Scholar." I am especially grateful to Prof. Yu Wenxuan, who gave me encouragement and suggestions for writing this book. I am indebted to Wang Xingxi and Bi Xinyu, two postgraduate students at the Central University of Finance and Economics. Without their efforts, I would be years behind in this book. They worked tirelessly to help me with the details associated with the survey and field trip. The team at Routledge, Lam Yong Ling and Payal Bharti, have been very supportive and efficient in editing this book. I am also grateful to my husband and daughter for their support and encouragement of my academic pursuits.

# 1    Introduction

Regional collaborative governance is one of the most important topics of public administration in recent years.[1] As for the metropolitan collaborative governance, the establishment and improvement of the mechanism of collaborative governance has become an important part of solving the regional public problems; On the other hand, due to the problem of "fragmentation" in regional governance, it is difficult to achieve a long-term and an effective collaboration between local governments in metropolitan region. How can local governments in metropolitan region collaborate with each other and construct a collaborative mechanism in order to maximize regional interests? These questions have become the issues of constant reflection and inquiry by scholars and government officials. Jan Jacobs wrote in her book *The Death and Life of Great American Cities*:

> Big cities have difficulties in abundance because they have people in abundance. But vital cities are not helpless to combat even the most difficult of problems.... Vital cities have marvelous innate abilities for understanding, communicating, contriving and inventing what is required to combat their difficulties. Perhaps the most striking example of this ability is the effect that big cities have had on disease. Cities were once the most helpless and devastated victims of disease, but they became great disease conquerors.[2]

If a city is indispensable to overcome the urban problems, the metropolitan region composed of several cities is indispensable to conquer and overcome the wider regional public problems, and the collaborative mechanism and model among them will determine the effectiveness of solving regional public problems.

## The definition of metropolitan coordinating region

At present, there are three related concepts about the definition of city area, namely metropolitan district, metropolitan area and megalopolis. These three concepts have their distinctive characteristics and connect with each other (see Table 1.1).

Governments and scholars in different countries have different definitions of metropolitan district. In Britain, it is called "metropolitan county," while it is called "urbanization area" in France, "urbanized area" in Germany and "statistical areas" in Australia.[3] In 1910, the United States formally adopted the concept of "metropolitan area," which refers to a central city with populations of more than 100,000 people or more than 100,000 people and an area connected to the central city with a population density of 1.5 million persons per square mile.[4] In 2000, after several modifications, the US government defined the latest metropolitan indicators system (Core Based Statistic Area, CBSA), that is, metropolitan district consists of three parts: (1) Central core area: Each metropolitan area index system has at least one urbanized area with a population of less than 50,000 or urban cluster with a population of no less than 10,000 defined by the census bureau. Urbanized areas and urban clusters are collectively referred to as urban areas; (2) Central county: It means that at least 50 percent of the population live in urban areas with a population size of not less than 10,000 people, or that at least 5000 people live in a single urban area with a population size of not less than 10,000 people; (3) Peripheral counties: it refers that the people living in the periphery counties but working in central counties occupies 25 percent of the total employment in the peripheral counties, or 25 percent of the employed population in the peripheral counties live in the central county.[5] Therefore, some scholars have pointed out that the definition of metropolitan areas in different countries is consistent in the perspective of spatial structure. They all include the core area (city center) and marginal zone (suburban county), and the specific indicators also covers the economic center (population size), economic hinterland (employment) and economic ties between the center and the hinterland (commuting rate).[6] Scholars in China argue that commuting rate is not the main mode of social and economic relation between urban and rural areas in China, and it cannot describe the characteristics of metropolitan area in China accurately. Thus, indicators of non-agricultural levels in the periphery areas can be used to define the metropolitan areas. For example, peripheral areas where non-agricultural output accounts for more than 75 percent of GDP, and non-agricultural labor force accounts for 50 percent or more than 60 percent of the social labor force can be defined as metropolitan areas.[7]

With regard to the total population of metropolitan district, some scholars believe that 500,000 people are more suitable, which is equivalent to the population of prefecture level cities in China.[8] Some scholars believe that more than 1 million people are more in line with the definition of metropolitan district,[9] and this study agrees with the latter. The spatial structure of metropolitan district has an obvious single center, and the agglomeration effect of central city is prominent. The service, control and management functions of cities are relatively centralized, and the central cities are mainly based on high-tech industries and service industries. The peripheral cities and counties mainly play the roles of industry, residence and leisure, and have high level of non-agricultural and urbanization.[10] Since the central cities of the metropolitan district and the peripheral counties are an organic whole with close social and economic links, and do not involve administrative issues across the administrative regions, it is easier to coordinate local governments in the region. China's Beijing, Tianjin, Shanghai and Chongqing are the most typical metropolitan districts.

The metropolitan area is a concept between metropolitan district and megalopolis. Japan put forward the concept of the metropolitan area in the 1960s, and the population size of the central city in the metropolitan area is more than 100,000, and the commuting rate of the peripheral areas to the central city should be more than 5 percent. In addition, the metropolitan area is divided into central metropolitan area and local metropolitan area. Among them, the central city of central metropolitan area is the city designated by the central government or the city with a population of more than 1 million. Besides, its adjacent area has some cities with a population of more than 500,000, the commuter population from the peripheral areas to the central cities is not less than 15 percent of the local population, and the volume of goods transported between metropolises shall not exceed 25 percent of the total volume of transportation.[11] Chinese scholars have pointed out that metropolitan area is an area of interregional structure consisting of one or more core cities and a number of towns and regions adjacent to but not affiliated with the core urban areas. In addition, Chinese scholars have stipulated that the population of the central city is more than 1 million, and that there are cities with a population of more than 500,000 nearby; The GDP of the central city should be higher than 45 percent; the central city has the urban function of crossing administrative area; the commuting rate from the peripheral to the central city is not less than 15 percent of the population.[12] As the core city of metropolitan area, metropolis plays an important role in the metropolitan area. Prof G. William Skinner argues that:

*Table 1.1* Comparison of some characteristics of metropolitan district, metropolitan area and megalopolis

| | | | |
|---|---|---|---|
| Population scale | The central city has a population of more than 1 million people | The population of the central city is greater than 1 million, and the secondary cities have a population of more than 500,000, with a total population of more than 5 million | The population of the central city is more than 4 million, and the secondary cities have a population of more than 1 million, with a total population of more than 25 million |
| Socio-economic characteristics | The non-agricultural added value of the peripheral counties of the central cities accounted for more than 75% of GDP. Non-agricultural employment accounts for 50%–60% of the total population of employment | The peripheral cities have close collaborative relationship with the central cities, and the GDP centrality of the central cities is greater than 45% | National political, economic and cultural core areas. Regional urbanization level is high, urban and rural is integrated |
| Agglomeration and diffusion effects | The agglomeration effect of central cities is obvious, showing the characteristics of single center | Single core or multi core, agglomeration and diffusion effect simultaneously | Mainly diffusion |

| *Organizational management characteristics* | The central city and the outlying counties are an organic whole, and the collaboration is relatively easy to be achieved | Crossing administrative boundaries. The collaboration among local governments is relatively difficult | Across several metropolitan circles. Horizontal cooperation is difficult, and it needs the national control |
| --- | --- | --- | --- |
| *Sketch map of spatial structure* |  |  | |

Data sources: Tao Xidong: "Trans Regional Governance: A New Approach to Economic Integration in China's Trans Provincial Metropolitan Coordinating Region," from *Geographical Science*, 2005 (5); XieShouhong: "The Definition and Comparative Analysis of Metropolitan Area, Metropolitan Coordinating Region and Urban Belt," from *Urban Issues*, 2008 (6); Chen Ruilian, Liu Yaping, et al. *Regional Governance Research: A Perspective of International Comparison.* page 177, Beijing, Central Compilation and Translation Press, 2013.

mega-cities are at the highest levels of the central hierarchy that are integrated in varying degrees. This hierarchy extends downward to rural towns.... As a result, the higher the hierarchy is, the more complex the social economic system is, among which the central area plays the role of connecting point.[13]

Therefore, "through the complex overlapping networks, each level of society and economic system is linked to a higher-level system. Large-area economies—such as the Pearl River Delta and the large area centered on the Chengdu Plain—can be seen as a hierarchical structure consisting of local and regional systems."[14] Metropolitan area is a multi-level, dynamic and open urban system, where the central city and the surrounding cities form a division of labor with vertical division of labor. The surrounding cities form a horizontal division of labor, so as to realize the regional integration results in terms of regional advantages and resources sharing, agglomeration and diffusion effect simultaneously.[15] The three metropolitan areas in Japan, Tokyo, Osaka and Nagoya, play an important role in Japan's economic and social development. However, due to the different parts consisting of the metropolitan area need to cross the boundaries of the administrative areas, the cooperation and coordination between local governments are rather difficult.

Megalopolis is a broader concept, also known as "urban agglomeration," "urban economic circle," "metropolitan circle" and so on. Some scholars point out that the development of American urbanization is a prerequisite for the emergence of megalopolis, and the megalopolis is the natural result of the development of metropolitan areas,[16] that is, the megalopolis is the organic integration or series of metropolitan areas, which is the result of spreading and blending the metropolitan areas in the same or adjacent region.[17] Chinese scholars have put forward that the megalopolis is a densely populated area with one or more cities as the core, with certain integration tendencies and layered spatial structure characteristics.[18] Some scholars believe that the megalopolis is a huge strip-shaped town corridor that is connected by several geographically adjacent metropolitan areas.[19] Furthermore, its total population is more than 25 million people, with the population of the central city more than 4 million, the secondary city more than 1 million people, and there are a large number of small and medium-sized cities and towns.[20] *The 2010 China Urban Agglomeration Development Report* released by the Institute of Geographical Science and Resources of the Chinese Academy of Sciences points out that, according to the standards of "there are not less than 3 metropolitan areas or big cities and at least one mega or super-large city as the core in the megalopolis," "the population size is not less than 20 million people," "the level of urbanization is greater than 50%, and the proportion of non-agricultural output exceeds 70%," "The per capita GDP exceeds US$3,000, and the economic density is greater than 5 million yuan RMB per square kilometer," China is forming 23 megalopolis.[21] Megalopolis make urbanization spread over vast areas. The intensive use of land, infrastructure sharing and urban-rural integration between different cities have obvious social and economic benefits, and thus occupy a central position in the political, economic, scientific and technological and cultural development of a country.[22] Because the megalopolis spans several metropolitan areas, horizontal cooperation within the region is more difficult and requires coordination at the national level.

Based on the above discussion, the definition of metropolitan area adopted in this study is mainly based on the scholars' basic definitions of "metropolitan areas," but it is not limited to the basic definitions. Combined with the concept of metropolitan district and megalopolis, the metropolitan area of this study mainly refers to a number of geographically adjacent cities or regions as the economic, social, cultural and ecological integration, in which one or more mega cities is the core. At present, Chinese and foreign scholars have different definitions of many quantitative indicators for metropolitan districts, metropolitan areas and megalopolis. Therefore, there is no substantive discussion and definition of the quantitative indicators (such as population size, geographical radius, etc.) in this study. This study mainly discusses the collaborative governance of the pearl river delta, Yangtze river delta and Beijing-Tianjin-Hebei region from the perspectives of organizational management.

## The "fragmentation" of governance in metropolitan area

The formation of metropolitan areas often depends on similar terrain, watershed and climate. Many metropolitan areas in the world are such a natural ecological whole, such as the Great Lakes metropolitan areas in North America and the London-centered metropolitan areas in Britain. As a result of the ecological integrity of the nature, the various administrative subjects in the metropolitan area need to cooperate in ecological management such as comprehensive watershed development, water resources management and air pollution. However, in reality, such ecological overall is divided into different administrative divisions, and various administrative subject have different levels of economic development, coupled with lack of policies and regulations and other factors, which causes the plight of cross-border public issues. In the arrangement of regional governance system, under the influence of planned economy system in a long time, the industrial isomorphism between cities in China is prominent, lacking the basis for mutual cooperation, and the fiscal and taxation system of "division of eating" has intensified the "administrative division" between cities. In the regional development of more than 30 years of reform and opening up, the phenomenon of "administrative district economy" has become prominent.[23] The "political tournament" mechanism promoted by local officials led to the "vassal economy,"[24] thus forming the vicious competition between the local governments.[25] Therefore, in the process of economic development, the competition among local governments is more than cooperation.

In recent years, the problems of water resource distribution, air pollution and cross-border river pollution in Beijing-Tianjin-Hebei, Yangtze River Delta, Pearl River Delta and other metropolitan areas in China have made intergovernmental cooperation in metropolitan areas an important issue that governments at all levels in the region must face. However, due to the continuous emergence of "fragmentation" or administrative segmentation in regional management,[26] the lack of cross-border administrative coordination mechanism,[27] the trust mechanism, interest coordination mechanism and evaluation mechanism,[28] it is difficult for local governments in metropolitan areas to achieve long-term and effective cooperation. In the aspect of metropolitan governance, especially in the Yangtze River Delta, Pearl River Delta and Beijing-Tianjin-Hebei region, the metropolitan local governments have encountered many problems.

First, the regional local governments have institutional obstacles in the governance of cross-border public affairs. Local governments are independent and lack of consideration for the overall regional interests; when making public policies, local governments often only consider the development goals of their jurisdiction in a short time, and the whole metropolitan area lacks an overall development goal and long-term planning. In this respect, the problem of cross-border water resources management in Beijing-Tianjin-Hebei is more prominent. Beijing-Tianjin-Hebei is a region with a shortage of water resources, and there is a contradiction between supply and demand in the distribution of water resources. For a long time, Hebei Province has undertaken the task of supplying production and domestic water for Beijing and Tianjin, especially Zhangjiakou and Chengde are the main water sources and ecological barriers for Beijing and Tianjin. However, while ensuring the water supply and water environment security in Beijing and Tianjin, some areas of Hebei Province are facing a series of ecological and environmental problems, such as the shortage of water supply and demand, soil erosion, land desertification and water pollution. Therefore, how to break the barriers of administrative divisions, effectively solve the coordinated water supply in the region, and formulate the development goals and strategic planning of water resources management in the region as a whole is an urgent issue to be solved.

Second, the existing collaboration and coordination mechanisms of regional local governments in cross-border public affairs are not complete. At present, the collaboration of local governments in China is lack of institutional framework, and there is no formal collaboration mechanism between regional governments. The cooperation between local governments often stays in the loose mechanism of bilateral mutual visits and multilateral consultations of senior executive heads. Although some institutionalized forms of regional cooperation have been gradually formed in Beijing-Tianjin-Hebei and the Yangtze River Delta, such as the "joint meeting of Mayors for economic cooperation in the Bohai Rim region" or the regional cooperation organization with independent office, such as the "Yangtze River Delta coordination meeting," the regional local governments have not been able to manage the ecological environment issues across the administrative regions, develop the overall resource strategy and major infrastructure construction.

Third, regional local governments are lacking cross regional collaboration organizations in cross-border public affairs. In the cooperation of local governments, there is a lack of an organization that represents the common interests of all parties, shares information of all parties, formulates regional public policies and implements regional planning. Therefore, it is difficult to effectively coordinate the relationship between the cities in the region in terms of cross administrative area public affairs, which in turn affects the actual implementation of regional public policies. Whether in the cross administrative areas of ecological environment governance, water resources distribution and management, public crisis emergency rescue work or in the collaboration of transportation and cultural industry, etc., there is a lack of a strong regional cooperation organization to coordinate and plan the overall development strategy and public policy of the region. For example, due to the lack of coordination of cross regional cooperation organizations such as the river basin environmental protection and governance committee, environmental pollution and ecological security problems in the Yangtze River Delta are becoming increasingly serious, especially in the Taihu Lake area, the drainage area accounts for only 0.38 percent of the country's total, while the emission volume is 10 percent of the country's total. Serious water environmental pollution makes the Taihu Lake Basin suffer from a common "water shortage."[29] For another example, the occurrence of sandstorms in Beijing-Tianjin-Hebei is largely due to the lack of regional coordination organizations, disordered competition and repeated construction between regional local governments and enterprises, which leads to serious damage to the regional ecological environment.[30]

In addition, the coordination among local governments in the region lacks the guarantee of legislation. At present, there is no institutional and legal guarantee for regional cooperation. Neither the central government nor the local government has issued corresponding laws and regulations to regulate cross regional public affairs cooperation and the rights and responsibilities of local governments in cooperation. This makes the regional cooperation between local governments lack of institutional and legal constraints, unable to form a conventional cooperation and coordination mechanism. The development of many metropolitan areas in the world is supported by a complete legal system. For example, the development of Tokyo Metropolitan Area in Japan is supported by national land development planning law, urban planning law and other laws, as well as local government laws and regulations on metropolitan area planning and local planning. Each level of regional and urban planning has specific laws as the guarantee of preparation and implementation, and the subjects involved in the planning should strictly implement the laws, so as to avoid the problem of incongruity between departments when implementing the planning.

Finally, the coordinated development of regional local governments depends on the good exchange of talent in the region. At present, many regions in China lack the platform of talent exchange, cooperation, training and sharing. In the division and cooperation of regional cultural industry, the flow of talent is particularly important. It is an important way to promote the coordinated development of regional cultural industry to establish a database of cultural industry talent, regularly release the demand information of cultural industry talent, promote the construction of talent intermediary organization and market, and create a good environment for the orderly flow of cultural industry talent. However, in these aspects, the work of local governments in various metropolitan areas in China is lagging behind. In addition, in the metropolitan area, the mutual recognition of cultural industry talent qualification certificates, the exchange and sharing of education, training and examination resources, and the unification of service standards have not been put on the agenda of local governments.

It is because of the above problems that the industrial relations within the metropolitan areas of China are not satisfactory, and the integration process needs to be further improved. At the same time, these problems in cooperation also affect the actual implementation of regional policies. In accordance with the massive economic development in the region, "fragmentation" is a serious problem, which cannot break through the obstacles of administrative divisions, and there is no substantive cooperation and coordination mechanism. Therefore, how to effectively promote the collaborative governance of local governments in the metropolitan area has become a key issue in the current regional coordinated development. In a sense, with the continuous progress of urbanization and regional integration in China, metropolitan areas or metropolitan areas are gradually formed, and the collaborative governance of metropolitan areas will become a major form of regional governance in the future. The purpose of this study is to analyze, respond to and solve the above problems from the perspective of holistic governance theory, build a holistic collaborative governance mechanism of local governments in metropolitan area, adapt to the requirements of the equalization of public resource allocation and public service provision concerned by the regional inclusive development, and maximize the overall interests of the region.

## Regional collaboration and holistic governance

Since the late 1990s, as a response to the "fragmentation" caused by the new public administration, holistic governance has become a new way of governance. Perri 6, a British scholar, believes that holistic governance is characterized by collaboration and integration, and emphasizes that the government should not only integrate the institutions and functions of various departments within the government, but also integrate the functions of the government, the private sector and non-profit organizations.[31] The theory of holistic governance was initially put forward based on the integration of the functions of various departments within the government. With the development of this theory, it began to focus on the collaboration between the governments, between the government and non-governmental organizations and between the private sectors. In this sense, the theory of holistic governance has important theoretical value for regional public management, especially for the governance of metropolitan area. The collaboration and integration of local governments advocated by the theory of holistic governance has become an important way to promote the governance of public affairs in metropolitan areas.

The theory and practice at home and abroad have proved that the lack of the concept and mechanism of holistic governance is one of the important reasons for the administrative segmentation, the instability of the collaborative relationship between regional local governments and even the low efficiency of cooperation in the governance of regional public affairs. In recent years, the Chinese scholarships have paid more and more attention to the cooperation of local governments in metropolitan areas. However, at present, there is no systematic study on the cooperation of local governments in metropolitan areas in regional governance from the perspective of holistic governance.

The purpose of this book is to analyze, respond to and solve the problems existing in the above regional governance from the perspective of holistic governance theory, build a holistic collaborative governance mechanism of local governments in the metropolitan area, adapt to the requirements of public resource allocation and equalization of public service provision concerned by regional inclusive development, and maximize the overall interests of the region. From the perspective of holistic governance, the research on the collaborative governance mode of local governments in the metropolitan area in China can not only deeply understand the problems in the collaboration of local governments in the metropolitan area, but also further explore the new mechanism of regional problem cooperation of local governments in the metropolitan area. Second, it deeply analyzes the principle and mechanism of cross regional collaboration organization of metropolitan area in China, as well as the collaborative mechanism of local government, private sector and non-governmental organizations in environmental protection, transportation, public health, water resource distribution and management and other cross-border public affairs, which can provide the metropolitan areas in China with policy suggestions.

Therefore, from the perspective of holistic governance, it has three innovative meanings in theory, method and practice to study the local government collaboration in metropolitan areas.

First, with the development and deepening of the theory and practice of metropolitan governance, the integrated collaborative governance mechanism will become the forefront of Chinese academic and practical fields. At present, the research on the overall collaborative governance mechanism of metropolitan area is relatively weak, so the research has the significance of theoretical expansion. Based on the integration of regional multi-party cooperative governance, integrated governance, complex network governance and other theories, this study aims at the problem of uncoordinated governance in metropolitan areas, closely follows the current dilemma of collaborative governance of public affairs in metropolitan area in China, and builds the theoretical framework of integrated collaborative governance of local governments in metropolitan area. From the perspective of central government, local government in metropolitan area, cross regional integrated cooperation organization, private sector, non-profit organization, this framework analyzes the theoretical issues such as collaborative mechanism of local government in metropolitan area, network structure of collaborative governance, and provides theoretical analysis for the diagnosis and optimization of collaborative governance of cross-border public issues in metropolitan area.

Second, on the basis of the theory of holistic governance, we should build a holistic collaborative governance mechanism of local governments in the metropolitan area to adapt to the inclusive development of our region. On this basis, through the social network analysis (SNA) and other empirical research, this book deploys the analysis of the structure and characteristics of the metropolitan collaborative governance network, the mechanism of the metropolitan collaborative governance, further expanded the holistic governance theory, and laid the foundation for further development of the regional local government collaborative governance research. In view of the limitations of the existing analytical methods of regional collaborative governance, this study transfers the social network analysis method to the analysis of metropolitan collaborative governance, and visualizes the relationship data that is difficult to quantify, and takes it as the methodological support of the empirical analysis of metropolitan collaborative governance network, so as to gradually analyze the relationship data according to the network density, point centrality, intermediate centrality and other variables. It is of innovative significance to analyze the structure and performance of metropolitan collaborative governance network.

Finally, according to the theoretical framework of the integrated and cooperative governance of the local governments in the metropolitan area, and by using the methods of social network analysis, this book analyzes the structure and characteristics of the collaborative governance network of cross-border public affairs in the metropolitan area, as well as the mechanism of the collaborative governance in the metropolitan area, and proposes to integrate and optimize the collaborative activities of the local governments from the perspective of the integrated governance for the cities of Beijing, Tianjin, Hebei, Yangtze River Delta, Pearl River Delta, etc. In order to realize long-term, stable and effective cooperation and realize regional coordinated development, it provides countermeasures and suggestions, so as to provide a new way for early warning, evaluation and monitoring of regional cross-border public affairs collaborative governance, and provide strong decision support for promoting the scientific regional strategic planning.

## The framework, methods and chapter outline of this book

### *Research framework*

In this study, the collaborative governance of metropolitan region dominated by holistic governance theory is a new trend in the form of regional cooperation between local governments, and the theoretical framework for analyzing the holistic collaborative governance of metropolitan area is proposed. The logical starting point of this analytical framework is the practical driving of regional government cooperation between regional governments and the analysis of the theory of metropolitan collaborative governance.

In practice, in view of the uncoordinated problems in the governance of the local governments in the metropolitan area, and in close touch with the current difficulties faced by the collaborative governance of the public affairs in the metropolitan area in China, this book analyzes the evolution of the regional spatial structure and the corresponding changes in the intergovernmental relations between the central government and the local government, and expounds the process from competition to cooperation of the local governments in the metropolitan area in China, that is, from the initial economic and technological cooperation, to the cooperation in metropolitan planning, then to the collaboration in dealing with the public affairs and the initial formulation of local government cooperation. In theory, based on the integration of regional multi-party collaborative governance, holistic governance, complex network governance and other theories, this study constructs a theoretical framework of integrated collaborative governance of local governments in metropolitan areas. This framework analyzes the cooperation mechanism and network structure of local governments in metropolitan areas from the dimensions of regional governments (central government or provincial government), local governments in metropolitan areas, cross regional collaboration organizations, private sector, non-profit organizations, etc., providing a theoretical framework for the diagnosis and optimization of cross-border public issues in metropolitan areas.

Second, on the basis of the theory of holistic governance, this book constructs a holistic collaborative governance mechanism of local governments in metropolitan area, that is, trust and communication mechanism, interest coordination and compensation mechanism, and supervision and evaluation mechanism, which adapts to the inclusive development of China's region. Through such integrated collaborative governance mechanism, the holistic governance mode of metropolitan area, which is composed of central government, local governments of metropolitan area, cross regional collaborative organization, non-profit organization and private sector, is established with the cross regional collaborative organization as the core. And through the social network analysis and other empirical research, the book completed the analysis of the structure and characteristics of the collaborative governance network for the public affairs, revised and adjusted the analytical framework of the holistic collaborative governance, further expanded the holistic governance theory, and laid the foundation for further research of the collaborative governance in local governments of metropolitan areas.

Third, through the analysis of collaborative governance of air pollution and neighborhood resistance in the process of urbanization in Beijing-Tianjin-Hebei metropolitan area, this book attempts to observe and recognize the overall collaborative governance mechanism and collaborative governance model of local governments in the metropolitan area from the practical level, and discuss the overall governance of the metropolitan area in a deeper level.

Finally, on the basis of theoretical, empirical and case studies, combined with the reality of the intergovernmental cooperation in contemporary China's metropolitan areas, and based on the theoretical framework of the holistic collaborative governance of local governments in metropolitan areas, this book completes the analysis of the collaborative governance mechanism, the holistic collaborative governance mode, and the cross-border public affairs collaborative governance in metropolitan areas by using methods including social network analysis, data visualization and research interviews. This study proposes to integrate and optimize the collaborative activities of local governments from the perspective of holistic governance, so as to provide countermeasures and suggestions for the long-term, stable and effective cooperation of Beijing-Tianjin-Hebei, Yangtze River Delta, Pearl River Delta and other metropolitan areas, as well as for the realization of regional coordinated development, and to provide suggestions for the regional strategic planning.

### *Research methods*

Based on the research framework of the holistic governance of local governments in metropolitan areas, the following research methods are adopted.

- Literature research. The literature research mainly focuses on the theory of holistic governance, regional collaborative governance and complex network governance, and extracts the key theoretical elements to form the theoretical basis of this study; meanwhile, it collects the formal collaborative agreement signed between the metropolitan governments and the data of interaction between cities in metropolitan area.
- Investigation and interview. According to the characteristics of the organizational structure, collaborative mechanism and mode of the local governments in the metropolitan area, the experts from the central government to the local governments in the relevant fields of regional planning and research are selected for semi-structured interviews, focusing on the current non-cooperation in the public affairs in

the metropolitan area and the signing of cooperation agreements, to ensure the authenticity and integrity of data sources. At the same time, in-depth interviews were conducted with some local government officials and business leaders to understand the collaborative governance in the governance of public affairs in the metropolitan area.

- Social network analysis. By using the method of social network analysis, the network density, point centrality, center centrality and proximity centrality of regional public affairs cooperation among 13 city governments in Beijing-Tianjin-Hebei metropolitan area from 2004 to 2011, such as ecological environment, transportation integration, cultural industry, public crisis emergency rescue, are measured and analyzed, and the structure, characteristics and performance of local government collaborative network in Beijing-Tianjin-Hebei metropolitan area is analyzed, which provide quantitative support for the analysis of the overall collaborative governance of local governments in Beijing-Tianjin-Hebei metropolitan area. At the same time, the data visualization technology is used to present the analysis results. Through the visualized cooperation network diagram and agglomerated sub group analysis diagram of Beijing-Tianjin-Hebei metropolitan area between the city governments described by the net draw drawing tool loaded by UCINET, the status of the internal composition structure of the metropolitan area and the interaction between the city members are revealed, and the evolution trend of the regional collaborative network of Beijing-Tianjin-Hebei is analyzed.
- Case study. Case study can effectively realize the in-depth study of individual and idiosyncratic problems. Through the analysis of the cases of air pollution in the collaborative governance of Beijing-Tianjin-Hebei metropolitan area and the case of NIMBY resistance in China's urbanization process, this study discusses the division of powers in the intergovernmental cooperation and the relationship between the government, citizens and society in the regional governance, so as to realize the deep understanding of collaborative governance of local governments in the metropolitan area.

## *Chapter outline*

This book takes the collaboration of local governments in the metropolitan area of China as the research object, focusing on the collaborative governance mechanism of local governments in the metropolitan area and the formulation of cross regional holistic collaborative organizations. On this basis, it puts forward the holistic collaborative governance mode of local governments in the metropolitan area, that is, integrating local governments, cross regional holistic collaborative organizations, non-governmental organizations and the private sector. The purpose of this book is to expand the current research on the collaborative governance of metropolitan area and provide an effective way for local governments to achieve long-term, stable and effective cooperation in regional public affairs.

This book tries to formulate the preliminary theoretical framework for the holistic governance of the local government in the metropolitan area. The book is composed of six chapters besides the introduction.

Chapter 1: As the beginning of the book, the introduction part discusses the definition of metropolitan area, the "fragmentation" of governance in metropolitan area, the necessity and entailing challenges for the local governments in collaborative governance of metropolitan area, the relationship between holistic governance and regional collaboration, and briefly introduces the main contents of each chapter of this book.

Chapter 2: The theoretical research of intergovernmental collaborative governance in metropolitan area. Based on the literature review of local government collaborative governance in metropolitan area, this chapter analyzes and summarizes three kinds of theories of local government collaboration in metropolitan area: metropolitan governance theory with regional multi-party cooperation as the leading role, metropolitan governance theory with complex governance network as the leading role and intergovernmental cooperation theory with holistic governance theory as the leading role. On this basis, it proposes that the collaboration and integration of local governments, which is advocated by the theory of holistic governance, is an important way to promote the governance of public affairs in the metropolitan area. As the theory of holistic governance is characterized by collaboration, integration and "cross-border," it emphasizes the cross sector collaboration in regional governance, focusing on the formation of collaborative mechanism among governments in the region, between governments and other social participants, and then attends to the overall interests, which play an important role in the collaborative governance of local governments in the metropolitan area. Therefore, this study takes "the theory of metropolitan governance dominated by regional multi-party cooperation" as an important research basis, the governance mechanism formed by "the theory of metropolitan governance dominated by complex governance network" as an important literature source, and focuses on analyzing, responding to and solving the cross-border public affairs collaboration of local governments in metropolitan areas from the perspective of "holistic governance." This book studies the operation of the holistic governance mechanism and the formulation of the collaborative organization of the local government in the metropolitan area,

constructs the theoretical framework of the holistic collaborative governance of the local government in the metropolitan area, and analyzes the
model of the holistic collaborative governance of the metropolitan area
which adapts to the inclusive development.

Chapter 3: Local government cooperation in the ecological governance
of metropolitan area: the affecting factors of collective action. Based on
the discussion of the theory of local government collaborative governance
in Chapter 2, this part discusses the affecting factors of the collective
action of local government in the ecological governance in China from the
perspective of the most prominent ecological problem in the collaborative
governance. It attempts to interpret the dilemma of Chinese ecological
governance cooperation from the perspective of institutional collective
action, and analyze how the common interest of local government ecological collaborative governance, the different preferences in overall objectives, the attributes of public goods in ecological governance, and the
imbalanced influence among cooperative members, promote or restrict the
collaboration of local governments in the metropolitan area and how the
political tournament of local officials in China over stimulates the "negative spillover" of ecological governance, while the stimulation of
"positive spillover" is not enough. Finally, it leads to the dilemma of cross
regional collaboration within the metropolitan area. Based on the analysis
of the typical case of the governance of the poverty belt around Beijing
and Tianjin, this study attempts to solve the dilemma of regional ecological governance in China. Based on the analysis of the affecting factors of
the intergovernmental cooperation in the ecological governance of the
metropolitan area, the collaborative mode in Chapter 4 is discussed.

Chapter 4: The integrated and collaborative governance mode of local
governments in metropolitan area. This chapter analyzes how to construct
the integrated collaborative governance model of metropolitan area, which
includes four parts: the integration of collaborative governance system and
the construction of information platform; the construction of cross regional
holistic collaborative organization; the establishment and improvement of
holistic collaborative governance mechanism; and the holistic collaborative network of metropolitan area. The integration of the administrative
management system of the local government in the metropolitan area is
inseparable from the construction of the regional information platform.
The establishment of the regional information sharing and exchange
platform, which connects the local government departments and the
government websites among the local governments, can create conditions
for breaking the barriers between the government and the departments
and realizing the rapid exchange between the local governments. The
key of local government collaboration in metropolitan area lies in the

construction of cross regional holistic collaborative organization, which is the organizational form of regional holistic governance. The construction of collaborative organizations should not only ensure the willingness and fairness of each local government member, but also ensure the legitimacy and authority of the organization itself, and have the right of financial distribution and management for the special funds of cross-border public affairs in the metropolitan area. The mechanism of trust and communication, interest coordination and compensation, supervision and evaluation among local governments, non-profit organizations and the private sector in metropolitan area is the link connecting the interaction of various subjects in metropolitan area, and also the way and channel for cooperation among them.

Chapter 5: Local government cooperation and regional inclusive development: an empirical analysis of social network based on Beijing-Tianjin-Hebei metropolitan area. Based on the theoretical research of the first four chapters on the holistic governance mode of the local government in the metropolitan area, this chapter uses the social network analysis method, taking the metropolitan area of Beijing-Tianjin-Hebei as an example, to make an empirical analysis on the collaborative network of 13 cities in Beijing, Tianjin and Hebei. Most of the researches on the relational network of local governments in metropolitan area are focused on the theory and framework of governance network, but there is no systematic research on the whole collaborative network and its evolution of local governments in metropolitan area. This chapter uses the social network analysis method to study this network, and attempts to analyze the structure, characteristics and evolution of the local government collaborative network from the aspects of network density, point centrality, intermediate centrality and proximity centrality, and discusses the evolution of the local government collaborative network in the metropolitan area, and proposes how to improve the governance performance of the local government collaborative network in the metropolitan area.

Chapter 6: This chapter summarizes the main contents of this book, and points out that the administrative segmentation in the collaborative governance of the local governments in the metropolitan area, as well as the lack of cooperative institutions and mechanisms and other problems lead to the local governments' difficulty in achieving effective collaboration. The cooperation, integration and "cross-border" advocated by the holistic governance, as well as the holistic governance network formed by various government departments, between the government and the government, between the government, the private sector and non-profit organizations, are of great significance for the solution of the collaborative governance problems and the achievement of the collaborative governance in the metropolitan area. After more than 30 years of competition and cooperation, local governments in metropolitan areas in China have formed basic forms of cooperation, such as collaboration and exchange, signing intergovernmental cooperation agreements, and regional counterpart support. However, due to the differences in the common interests and overall preferences of the local governments in the metropolitan area, the uneven influence among the cooperative members, and the political tournament mode for the local officials and other factors, the collaboration of local governments in the metropolitan area is restricted. Building the trust and communication mechanism, benefit distribution and compensation mechanism, supervision and evaluation mechanism of metropolitan area, and based on these mechanisms, the holistic collaborative governance mode of metropolitan area, which is composed of collaborative governance information platform, cross regional holistic collaborative organization and collaborative governance network, is an important way to achieve the holistic governance of metropolitan area. Through the analysis of the social network of 13 cities in Beijing-Tianjin-Hebei metropolitan area, this book further verifies and confirms the importance of building the mechanism and model of urban collaborative governance, and puts forward the process of long-term, stable and effective collaboration in China's metropolitan area. We should further coordinate the intergovernmental relations between the central government and the local government and between the local government and the local government, establish a unified information network system in the metropolitan area, build an integrated cross regional collaborative organization, improve the ecological compensation mechanism of the local government in the metropolitan area, and build a multi governance mechanism for the overall collaboration of the local government in the metropolitan area.

## Notes

1 See H. V. Savitch, "Territory and Power: Rescaling for a Global Era Proceedings of the International," *Proceedings of the International Conference on Urban and Regional Development in the 21st Century*, Sun Yat-sen University, December 17–18, 2011; Chen Ruilian et al., *Study on Theory and Practice of Regional Public Management*. (Beijing: China Social Science Press, 2008).
2 Jane Jacobs, *The Death and Life of Great American Cities*. (New York: Random House, 1961), 447.
3 See Wang Xu, Luo Sidong, *Local Government in the New Urbanization Period of the United States: The Game Between Regional Coordination and Local Autonomy*. (Xiamen University Press, 2010), 43–44.
4 Ibid., 3.
5 See Luo Haiming, Tang Jin, Hu Lingqian and Wang Jie, "New Progress in Defining Index Systems in Metropolitan Areas of the United States," *Foreign Urban Planning*, 2005 (3).

6 See Wang Xu, Luo Sidong: *Local Government in the New Urbanization Period of the United States: The Game Between Regional Coordination and Local Autonomy.* (Xiamen University Press, 2010), 45.

7 See Hu Xuwei, Zhou Yixing et al., *Study on Spatial Agglomeration and Diffusion of China's Coastal Cities and Towns.* (Beijing: Science Press, 2000); Xie Shouhong: "Conceptual Definition and Comparative Analysis of Metropolitan Area, Metropolitan Coordinating Region and Metropolitan Belt," *Urban Issues*, 2008 (6).

8 See Xie Shouhong, "Conceptual Definition and Comparative Analysis of Metropolitan Area, Metropolitan Coordinating Region and Metropolitan Belt," *Urban Issues*, 2008 (6).

9 See Tao Xidong, *Study on the Economic Analysis and Integration Mechanism of the Administrative Region of Trans-provincial Metropolitan Area—A Case Study on Xuzhou Metropolitan Area*, Doctoral Dissertation of East China Normal University, 2004.

10 See Xie Shouhong, "Conceptual Definition and Comparative Analysis of Metropolitan Area, Metropolitan Coordinating Region and Metropolitan Belt," *Urban Issues*, 2008 (6).

11 See Wei Wei and Zhao Guangrui, "A Review of the Patterns of Metropolitan Coordinating Region in Japan," *Modern Japanese Economy*, 2005 (2).

12 See Zhang Jingxiang, Zou Jun, "A Study on the Organization of Regional Space in Metropolitan Coordinating Region," in *Urban Planning*, 2001 (5); Zhang Wei, "Concept, Characteristics and Planning of Metropolitan Coordinating Region," in *Urban Planning*, 2003 (6); Tao Xidong, "Trans Regional Governance: A New Approach to Economic Integration in China's Trans Provincial Metropolitan Coordinating Region," in *Geographical Science*, 2005 (5).

13 G. William Skinner, *The City of Late Chinese Empire.* (Beijing: China Publishing House, 2000), 2.

14 Ibid., 2–3.

15 See Xie Shouhong, "Conceptual Definition and Comparative Analysis of Metropolitan Area, Metropolitan Coordinating Region and Metropolitan Belt," *Urban Issues*, 2008 (6).

16 See Chen Ruilian, Liu Yaping et al., *Regional Governance Research: A Perspective of International Comparison.* (Beijing: Central Compilation and Translation Press, 2013), 177.

17 See GuoJiulin: "A Comprehensive Survey of the American Metropolitan Belt and its Implications," *Economic Geography*, 2008 (2).

18 Fan Jie, *Research on Regional Comprehensive Planning of Beijing Tianjin Hebei Metropolitan Coordinating Region.* (Beijing: Science Press, 2008), 65.

19 See Tao Xidong: "Trans Regional Governance: A New Approach to Economic Integration in China's Trans Provincial Metropolitan Area," *Geography Science*, 2005 (5).

20 See Xie Shouhong, "Conceptual Definition and Comparative Analysis of Metropolitan Area, Metropolitan Coordinating Region and Metropolitan Belt," *Urban Issues*, 2008 (6).

21 15 standard urban agglomerations of the 23 urban agglomerations are: The Yangtze River Delta, Pearl River Delta, Beijing Tianjin Hebei, The Shandong Peninsula, Liaodong Peninsula, the west side of the Straits, Changsha Zhuzhou Xiangtan, Wuhan, Chengdu and Chongqing, Poyang Lake Ring, The Central Plains, Harbin Dalian Changchun, Jianghuai, Guanzhong, Northern slope of

Tianshan mountains; The 8 urban agglomerations that are not up to standard are: North and South Qin Fang, Jinzhong, Yinchuan Plain, Hubaoe urban agglomeration, Jiayu Wine, Lan Bai Xi, Central Guizhou and Central Yunnan. See Zhong Xin, "China is Forming 23 Urban Groups Yangtze River Delta has become the world's top six," *Beijing Times*, 28.03.2012.

22  See Xie Shouhong, "Conceptual Definition and Comparative Analysis of Metropolitan Area, Metropolitan Coordinating Region and Metropolitan Belt," *Urban Issues*, 2008 (6).

23  See Liu Junde, "An Analysis of the Phenomenon of 'Administrative Region Economy' Highlighted in the Transition Period of China," *Theoretical Front*, 2004 (10).

24  See Zhou Lian, "A Study of the Promotion Model of Local Officials in China," *Economic Study*, 2007 (7).

25  See Zhou Lian, "The Encouragement and Cooperation of Government Officials in Promotion Game—Also on the Long-standing Causes of Local Protectionism and Repeated Construction in China," *Economic Research*, 2004 (6).

26  See Liu Junde, "An Analysis of the Phenomenon of 'Administrative Region Economy' Highlighted in the Transition Period of China," *Theoretical Front*, 2004 (10); Shu Qing, Zhou Keyu, *From Closure to Openness: Perspective of Chinese Administrative Economy*. (Shanghai, East China Normal University Press, 2003).

27  See Yang Long and Peng Yanqiang, "Understanding the Cooperation of Local Government in China—from the Perspective of Administrative Jurisdiction Transfer," *Study on Politics* 2009 (4); Wang Jian, Bao Jing, Liu Xiaokang, Wang Dianli, "The Proposition of 'Compound Administration'—A New Idea to Solve the Conflict between Regional Economic Integration and Administrative Division in Contemporary China," *Administrative Management of China*, 2004 (3).

28  See JinTaijun, "From Administrative Region Administration to Regional Public Management: A Game Analysis of the Evolution of Government Governance," *The Chinese Social Sciences*, 2007 (6); Yang Aiping, "From Vertical Incentive to Parallel Incentive: Incentive Mechanism for Local Government Cooperation," *Academic Research*, 2011 (5); Yu Gangqiang, CaiLihui, "A Study on the Networked Governance Model of Chinese Urban Agglomerations," *Administrative Management of China*, 2011 (6).

29  See Yao Xianguo, Xie Xiaobo, "The Analysis of the Competition Behavior of Local Government in the Economic Integration of Yangtze River Delta," *Journal of the Party School of the CPC Zhejiang Provincial Committee*, 2004 (3).

30  See Ma Hailong, "History, Present Situation and Future: On Regional Cooperation in Beijing, Tianjin and Hebei Province," *Economist*, 2009 (5).

31  Perri 6, Diana Leat, Kimberly Seltzer and Gerry Stoker, *Towards Holistic Governance: The New Reform Agenda*. (New York: Palgrave, 2002).

# 2    Theoretical research on intergovernmental collaborative governance in metropolitan area

Collaborative governance of local governments in a metropolitan area is not only an important component of regional public management, but also an area of public management to be expanded and deepened. After the new public management movement, with the development of regional governance theory and practice, the theory of collaborative governance in metropolitan area is booming, and a large number of research results have been produced. From the early twentieth century to 1960s, the consolidation of local governments had been used as an advanced basic mechanism to solve the plight of metropolitan areas in providing public services. Later, this mechanism was gradually replaced by multi-level, overlapping government and decentralized community control,[1] and solutions based on reshaping government oriented public entrepreneurship and innovative communities.[2] In recent decades, in order to solve the dilemma in the management of metropolitan areas, the "new regionalism" rises, which advocates the formation of a collaborative mechanism between different levels of government, non-governmental organizations and the private sector through negotiation, in order to jointly govern regional public affairs. At present, scholars have carried out in-depth research on local government cooperation in urban agglomerations, the collaborative governance model in metropolitan areas, and the application of institutional collective action framework in regional governance.[3] At the same time, as a new public governance approach after the new public management, the application of holistic governance in regional collaborative governance has become a new field of public management research.

At present, the academic research on the collaboration of local governments in metropolitan area mainly focuses on the following three aspects: The first is the governance theory of metropolitan area dominated by regional multi-party cooperation; the second is the governance theory of metropolitan area dominated by complex governance network; the third is the intergovernmental cooperation theory dominated by the holistic governance theory. This chapter will focus on these three aspects to make a systematic review and comment on the relevant literature of the theory of intergovernmental collaborative governance in the metropolitan area.

## The governance theory of metropolitan area dominated by regional collaboration

The theory of metropolitan governance, which is dominated by regional multi-party collaboration, advocates the formation of collaborative mechanism among different levels of government, social groups and private sectors in metropolitan area through negotiation, so as to jointly solve regional public affairs. This paradigm tries to find a balance between the "government model" dominated by "state intervention" and the "multi-center governance model" dominated by "market."

In the process of studying the collaborative governance of metropolitan area, the discussion about "regionalism" and "New Regionalism" has always been the focus of academic debates. The development of regionalism has gone through three stages: the first stage is devoted to strengthening the dominant power of the central city government through structural adjustment; the second stage emphasizes how the dominant power of the central city government gives way to the multi-center regional governance model; the third stage, namely the new regionalism, emphasizes the development of the government's governance ability rather than the expansion of the government itself. Allan D. Wallis, an American scholar, on the basis of studying the governance structure of metropolitan area, argues that the new regionalism is characterized by cross sector (public sector, private sector, non-profit organization) alliance, and advocates the formation of collaborative network among different levels of governments, social groups and private sectors in metropolitan area through negotiation, so as to jointly solve regional public affairs. However, because this network does not emphasize the government's leading role and lacks the corresponding government authorization, it limits the ability of solving and coordinating regional public affairs.[4]

The core problem of regional governance is how to resolve the collective action dilemma of local governments in the region and promote cross regional governance between cities. Scholars' attention to this issue has formed different theoretical paradigms, such as traditional regionalism, public choice theory, new regionalism, etc., and there have been "big box" model, "multi-level government" model, multi-center public choice model, "multilateral joint governance" model, urban community model, "leaping" cooperation model and other forms of regional collaborative governance.[5]

## The traditional theory of regionalism

The "big box" model and the "multi-level government" model are formed under the influence of traditional regionalism, emphasizing the establishment of new levels of government and vertical bureaucratic regulations. Traditional regionalism holds that it is necessary to strengthen the dominant power of central city government through structural adjustment. To solve the fragmentation problem of metropolitan governance, it is necessary to cancel the independent municipal governments in the region, and merge them into a huge and unified metropolitan government through the city county consolidation, in order to obtain the justice and fairness of social governance in the region. This mode is also called the "big box" mode, that is to say, replace the "small box" (the various municipal governments in the region) with the "big box" of the region (unified metropolitan government). This model is considered to be able to better absorb the externalities of the economy and the consequent spillover effect. The assumption of the "merging" model is that a unified and integrated regional government is more effective than a single municipal government in formulating and providing public policies and coordinating policy implementation. Therefore, it can better deal with the problems of the self-governance and the unequal distribution of resources in regional governance. Supporters of the "big box" model believe that this "big government" model can expand economies of scale and provide cheaper and more effective services to the people in the region. However, there are also practical difficulties in the "big box" model. First, local governments in the region may not be able to form a unified metropolitan government for their own interests. Second, even if local governments agree to establish a unified metropolitan government, such a regional government involves many changes in administrative divisions, which requires the central government's consent and approval.

The multi-level government is also one of the ways to solve the dilemma of urban governance. The core idea of this approach is to establish a government "umbrella level" to retain the independence of each city in the metropolitan area, but each city has transferred a certain degree of power to establish a higher level of metropolitan government, and achieve greater collaboration among different local governments. The "multi-level government" model is more flexible than the "big box" model. It divides the regional local government and metropolitan government in the area of social affairs management, and advocates that the local affairs should be solved by the regional local government, and the regional affairs should be solved by the metropolitan government. Local governments are responsible for relatively "narrow" local services, such as public security, health, housing and other matters that residents have to deal with every day; metropolitan governments are responsible for more extensive public affairs across different local government boundaries, such as formulating strategic plans and environmental protection, solid waste treatment and other ecological governance issues. Minneapolis in the United States adopted this way of governance. This model is considered to be able to respond to the needs of the people better and faster.[6]

Although the "big box model" and "multi-level government model" seem to coordinate the different goals of local government and regional government, they also face many obstacles in practice. Officials at the upper level are unhappy with officials in the middle tier government, who can direct a large area of constituency citizens in the region and exceed their authority. The bottom level government also does not like to accept the instructions of the metropolitan government. For example, the metropolitan government will ask the local government to take collaborative governance measures to build waste incineration plants or affordable housing for low-income people in the local government's region. Although these measures are beneficial to the whole metropolitan area, local governments are often reluctant to follow such orders for their own benefit. Therefore, the regional governance model advocated by traditional regionalism seems to be perfect in theory, but it cannot last for a long time in practice.

From the practice of regional governance in foreign countries, many metropolitan areas in North America, Europe and Asia have gone through three stages: building metropolitan government (structural reform), abolishing metropolitan government and regional governance movement.[7] In this process, many countries have established metropolitan governments in charge of regional affairs, such as the General Administration of Greater London, Tokyo metropolitan government, Toronto metropolitan government, Rotterdam metropolitan government and Washington metropolitan government. However, in practice, the metropolitan government has many drawbacks in managing regional affairs. For example, it is difficult to break through the shackles of the bureaucratic system to fully perform its functions, and it is difficult to establish the authority of governance in the region in a short time. Therefore, the metropolitan areas of some countries began to turn to the regional governance mode, in which the government worked with private enterprises and non-governmental organizations to jointly manage regional public affairs.

### Public choice theory

Public choice model is a multi-center voluntary model of collaboration. Different from the traditional regionalism, the public choice model believes that people can freely choose the areas that can best meet their own preferences to settle down, and these areas often can provide the public services that people need most. This mode is also known as "voting with your feet." So the theory of public choice thinks that the problem of "local fragmentation" in the region is exactly a positive point, because it can ensure the competition between local governments, so that the people can choose an optimal set of services.[8] Of course, the public choice model from the multicentric school mainly emphasizes the implementation of governance by relying on individual decisions under the conditions of market economy, with less attention to the collaboration of the public sector on regional issues. However, in dealing with public affairs, the government's intervention and management is essential, so it is difficult to cope with the governance of regional public affairs simply by relying on the public choice mode of "vote by feet." For example, for environmental protection, the central government and the state (provincial) government often require the cooperation among the governments in the region to prevent the spread of pollution and restore the clean air, which makes the public choice model face difficulties in the cooperation of regional governance.

The cooperation of many cities in the United States is regarded as the representative of multi-center public choice mode, such as Pittsburgh and Los Angeles. This type of city is called a diffuse metropolis. The diffuse metropolis model implies a large number of independent local governments nested in the background of metropolis. This type of metropolitan area usually contains a major city as the center of a "solar system," surrounded by small satellite cities. This system is changeable and asymmetric, so its cooperation is gradual and realized through governance rather than management. Some scholars describe these metropolises as diverse, overlapping, cross cutting and special functions of local governments. From the public's point of view, this means that the same family will receive services from different local governments. An ideal picture is that the city government is responsible for providing some necessary services (public security, roads and sanitation); the SAR government provides some special services (water, education); the larger regional government provides another set of services (social security, vehicle registration); the state (province) or the state maintains supervision of other services (environment, bridges and tunnels).[9] As a result, the metropolitan area is often described as "fragmented" and criticized as a seemingly incomprehensible "quilt made of rags" composed of local governments in the region. Of course, the defenders of multicentrism believe that the real life of the metropolitan area is not chaotic and balkanized, but a flexible collaborative network established by using agreements and contracts between local governments. Based on this, there is a call for "governance without government."

## New regionalism theory

"Multilateral joint governance" model, urban community model and "Leaping" collaboration model are the regional governance models formed under the influence of new regionalism, emphasizing the establishment of horizontal intergovernmental collaboration based on the existing government, trying to solve the conflicts of different administrative regions. The interaction of local interests and the consensus among them are regarded as the best way to reduce "negative externalities."

The new regionalism tries to find a balance between the traditional regionalism dominated by government intervention and the public choice theory dominated by market. It is characterized by a cross-sectoral (public sector, private sector, non-profit organizations) alliance, which advocates the formation of collaboration network among different levels of government, non-governmental organizations and private sector in metropolitan area through negotiation to jointly resolve regional public affairs.[10] The difference between the new regionalism and the traditional "big box model" is that the former emphasizes governance while the latter emphasizes management. The new regionalism theory advocates "to replace the single rigid government management mode with flexible horizontal governance network, and to absorb other non-profit organizations, business associations and civil organizations in the region to participate in the overall governance."[11] At the same time, the theory also tries to avoid the problems of local governments' low efficiency caused by the "multi-center" public choice mode, and tries to advocate regional integration and coordinated development through flexible policy network, and promote the construction of regional cooperation organizations.

Under the influence of the new regionalism theory, the urban governments in Europe and North America also explore new ways to solve the regional governance dilemma in practice. The "linked function" model is one of them. This model refers to the "docking" of functions between different governments in the governance of regional issues, or the signing of cooperation agreements between regions. Unlike the "big box" mode and the "multi-level government" mode, the "multilateral joint governance" mode is more flexible because it does not generate new government levels. During a period of time, the function of connectivity can be increased, deleted or transferred between different governments. Louisville in the United States has adopted this approach of governance. This mode not only preserves the autonomy of local governments, but also ensures the central city's leading role in regional governance. Of course, the flexibility of "Multilateral Governance" mode is often offset by its instability, in that only certain functional connections cannot achieve comprehensive and integrated intergovernmental cooperation. This pattern is often regarded as an expedient measure or a transitional stage toward the merger mode. In addition, the docking of functions advocated by this model will sometimes be affected by factors such as power distribution. Therefore, such functional connections will not necessarily lead to better management results.[12]

The urban community is also one of approaches of the regional governance influenced by new regionalism. This approach only brings together many local governments to collaborate without the need to establish a particular metropolitan government. The urban community maintains the integrity of local governments by merging local government officials into a metropolitan council. Metropolitan council has been given the responsibility of managing inter-regional issues such as environment, transportation and most importantly, it also imposes common taxes on local governments to achieve the common goals of the community. In this way, the urban community model is similar to the multi-level government mode, but this model does not exceed the authority of various local governments in terms of identity and election. It emphasizes the existing institutions and flexible institutional arrangements from the collaboration of local governments, so that the urban community model is to some extent a "hybrid" of "management" and "governance."[13] Because of this, urban community is probably the most flexible of these models. The city of Lyon in France and the city of Montreal in Canada have adopted this mode.

In addition, in the context of globalization, there are also innovative collaboration modes between cities that are not adjacent to each other, namely, collaboration of "jumped scales." This approach is a long-term collaborative relationship formed by an alliance between geographically non-contiguous regions, crossing national boundaries or state (province) regions.[14] In practice, the "Pan Pearl River Delta" regional cooperation in China, including Hong Kong, Macao, Guangdong, Fujian, Jiangxi and other inland provinces nearby is a typical cooperation of Jumped Scales model. In Europe, the cooperation between Marseille of France, Geneva of Switzerland and Barcelona of Spain also belongs to such mode of cooperation.

Under the influence of new regionalism, many forms of collaboration among local governments advocate that on the basis of local governments' voluntary participation in regional governance, many independent local governments in the region should be united through multiple networked agreements or contracts between regions to realize the collaboration of public affairs in the metropolitan area. These models emphasize the horizontal cooperation and linkages between local governments. The multiple networked services provided by many local governments means that people can choose the appropriate government services according to their own needs and situations. In this way, the multiple networked services provided by local governments in the region are targeted and expand the range of people's choice and participation. However, these governance models influenced by new regionalism also encounter many difficulties. First of all, there is no core government to guide the system, so it cannot ensure the solution of regional public problems; second, because this model emphasizes the self-governance of local governments, it is difficult to reach an agreement on the overall objectives of the region. As a result, it is easy to lead to the introduction of hasty and messy regional policies. In addition, these models ignore the collective responsibility, and no subject in the region can take full responsibility for the public issues of the region as a whole.

In a word, the "big box" model and the multi-level government model are more similar to the "government model." They emphasize the establishment of new government levels and vertical bureaucratic regulations; the "multilateral joint governance" model, the urban community model and the "Leaping" cooperation model are the establishment of horizontal intergovernmental collaboration based on the existing government; the public choice model is a multi-center voluntary cooperation model, so they are closer to the "governance model" (see Figure 2.1). "Management mode" and "governance mode" have their own focus on regional governance. The "big box" model attempts to address regional imbalances through democratic ways of command and control; while the multi-level government model attempts to find a balance between centralization and decentralization through diversified ways to better address the regional public issues within the scope. The multilateral joint governance model

| Monocentric ← | | | | | → Polycentric |
|---|---|---|---|---|---|
| Traditional Regionalism | | New Regionalism | | | Polycentricism |
| Consolidation | Multi-tiered | Collected jurisdictions | Urban Communities | Jumped Scales | Public Choice |

Government ← → Governance

*Figure 2.1* A continuum of re-scaled territories.

Source: H. V. Savitch, "Territory and Power: Rescaling for a Global Era," *Proceedings of the International Conference on Urban and Regional Development in the 21st Century*, Sun Yat-sen University, December 17–18, 2011.

tries to solve the conflicts of different administrative regions, and advocates the cooperation among different governments in the region; the community model, "Leaping" cooperation model and other new regionalism governance models believes that the interaction of local interests and the consensus among them is the best way to reduce negative externalities; the public choice model relies on the choices individuals make in a market economy. Although these models play a certain role in urban governance in the United States, they also have their own limitations. For example, the merger model and the multi-level government model face difficulties in how to determine the status of new governments and its authority. Another example refers to the public choice model which is characterized with little or no government involvement. It is difficult for this model to deal with cross-border public affairs in metropolitan areas simply relying on the "voting by foot" because government intervention and management are indispensable when dealing with public affairs.

Although the above-mentioned regional governance models provide theoretical resources for analyzing regional governance in China, none of them can fully explain the practice and innovation of regional collaboration in China. For example, China's regional collaboration will be strongly supported and intervened by the central government through national policies which can promote the development of the region. While under the federal constitutional system, the central government's participation in United States and many European countries is limited.

In recent years, Chinese scholars have also begun to pay attention to the governance of the metropolitan area and have conducted pioneering research on intergovernmental relationship and regional collaborative governance of China both in theory and practice. First, some scholars explored couple of important relationships in China, including the relationship between central government and local government, the relationship among local governments, and the position and direction of the relationship between various government departments.[15] As the negative impact of China's inter-regional development gap on social and economic development is becoming increasingly prominent, how to narrow the regional development gap and promote regional development has also become a major topic in China's regional governance research. The promotion of regional integration, cooperation and competition among regional governments, and regional coordinated development have gradually become the focus of scholars. Therefore, some scholars have suggested that China should shift from "district administration" to regional public management, and then from regional public management to regional governance.[16] With the rise of regional public problems, the "district administration" has increasingly exposed its inherent limitations and deficiencies, so it is necessary to construct a new form of government governance, that is, the regional public administration, to complement it.[17] Some Chinese scholars believe that the establishment of a cross-border joint government is more suitable for administrative organization and management system reform in China's current metropolitan areas after analyzing the existing problems of the administrative system of China's metropolitan areas.[18] Some scholars put forward the concept of regional "compound administration" on the theoretical level and considered it to be a new way to solve the regional economic integration and conflicts of administrative divisions in China. They also emphasize the cooperation of cross-administrative zoning and inter-administrative level between different governments and encouraging non-governmental organizations to participate in regional governance, thus forming a multi-center and self-governing collaborative mechanism through overlapping and nesting.[19] Some scholars believe that the regional governance advocated by the new regionalism has important significance for solving the public affairs problems in China's metropolitan area.[20] In recent years, while continuing the research of "new regionalism" theory, China's regional governance theory has been influenced by other theories such as "holistic government" and "networked governance" theory. After experiencing the changes of the post new public management era, the practice of the region's vigorous development represented by the Pearl River Delta, the Yangtze River Delta and the Beijing-Tianjin-Hebei region urgently needs the guidance of new regional theory. Therefore, some scholars have proposed to achieve cross-sectoral unified assistance and collaborative governance between different governments to build a networked governance platform.[21]

Specifically, scholars have conducted extensive research from different perspectives concerning the collaboration of local governments in the metropolitan area in the process of regional integration. They believe that China's regional government collaboration is a rational choice for regional economic integration in the existing system. To build a regional government collaborative mechanism, a good institutional environment, reasonable organizational arrangements and systematized collaborative rules are necessary.[22] Obviously, regional competition is the first problem needed to be solved for regional integration. Many researches provide a systematic perspective and framework for understanding China's regional economic competition and collaboration, conducing to explain the long-standing local protectionism, the "big and comprehensive" regional development strategy and the various industries competition between regions which leads to vicious competition.[23] Some scholars also analyze the local government competition from the political and market dimensions of intergovernmental competition.[24] Therefore, some scholars have proposed that the essence of regional public management is the institutional change in the way of governance, that is, breaking the institutional arrangement of the original administrative district and reshaping the institutional evolution of the interest pattern. In this process, there is always a game of different stakeholders. For all possible game dilemmas, governments at all levels should possess a "repetitive game" thinking of cooperation, establish information communication mechanism and bilateral or multilateral negotiation mechanism, cut off the interest relationship between local governments and the social-economic stakeholders, etc. As a result, the local governments need to establish a regional public management system to achieve effective guidance for the transformation of governance.[25] In the process of cooperation between local governments, the bargaining of cooperation should reach a consensus through transferring administrative jurisdiction between local governments. The reason lies that as a tool for cross-administrative affairs governance, the core role of cooperation between local governments is to form a regional public management power through the transfer of administrative jurisdiction to govern the cross-administrative public affairs.[26] Some scholars have suggested that China's current regional cooperation is only a purely government management, lacking the participation of many stakeholders. To further improve the quality of regional collaboration, it is necessary to improve existing regional cooperation strategies in a timely manner, enhancing communications between local governments and social stakeholders including enterprises and NGOs to form collaborative governance of multiple stakeholders in the region.[27]

Scholars have also conducted preliminary discussions on the model and mechanisms of regional collaboration. The regional local government collaboration model can be divided into six types: the EU inter-governmental cooperation mode) under the "Regional Network Governance," the GMS ("Greater Mekong Sub-region") government cooperation model, the government cooperation model in the Rhine River Basin governance, the "Oresund" regional cooperation model between Denmark and Sweden, the "Pan-Pearl River Delta" regional government cooperation model under the "one country, two systems" principle, and the mayor joint conference system model.[28] In addition, contract administration is an innovation of intergovernmental cooperation model in current China, and intergovernmental contract is the institutional support for contract administration. There are many differences and even essential differences in the pursuit of goals, basic attributes, contract subjects and implementation principles of the two models.[29] With the deepening of research, Chinese scholars have also increased the research on the collaborative mechanism between local governments in the metropolitan area. They believe that

China's local collaborative mechanism under developmental localism is a vertical incentive mechanism which is based on administrative decentralization, fiscal decentralization and political tournament. As a result, it faces some difficulties such as the incompatibility of internal and external incentives, political mobilization rather than equal game incentive. Therefore, a reasonable interest incentive mechanism is the institutional basis for realizing long-term cooperation among local governments. The high-level government should construct a parallel incentive mechanism covering the interest distribution, interest coordination, interest compensation and interest transfer among local governments through guidance and coordination, so as to realize a kind of institutionalized cooperation with equal status, autonomy and interest compatibility.[30] Based on the analysis of a series of limitations of regional government cooperation under the leadership of the central government, some scholars have proposed that the cooperation and coordination among China's regional governments in the future can be achieved through three ways below: horizontal accountability between local governments, vertical accountability from central government toward local governments, and accountability mechanism involving various civil society organizations and social forces.[31]

On the practical level, the development of urbanization and regional integration in China has promoted the development of metropolitan areas and urban agglomerations, and the governance of such areas has gradually become the focus of Chinese scholars, who have done some preliminary research. Scholars have conducted special research on the Pearl River Delta, the Yangtze River Delta, Beijing-Tianjin-Hebei, Changsha-Zhuzhou-Xiangtan and other regions. As the earliest region promoting the regional integration in China, the Pearl River Delta is an area where scholars have paid attention for a long time. Not only did they analyze the background and current situation of government cooperation in the Pan-Pearl River Delta region from the perspective of regional public management, but also explore the innovation and path of Pan-Pearl River Delta regional government cooperation in five aspects: cooperation concept, cooperation model, cooperation mechanism, cooperation norms and cooperation policies.[32] They also proposed that to effectively solve the governance dilemma in the process of regional integration development in the Pearl River Delta, it is necessary to achieve innovation in regional public management systems in terms of innovative institutional environment, diversification of governance mechanisms, regulation of governance entities,[33] and strengthen the role of enterprises, individuals and NGOs in promoting the evolution of urban agglomeration governance structure.[34] The Yangtze River Delta region is one of the earliest areas for regional cooperation in China. Actions—such as improving the Yangtze River

Delta regional cooperation mechanism, establishing the Yangtze River Delta Development Promotion Fund and strengthening the state's guidance on regional cooperation—will further promote regional development and cooperation in the Yangtze River Delta.[35] Some scholars pointed out that under the rapid development of globalization, regional economic integration is the trend of the times. The integration process in the Yangtze River Delta is the fastest, followed by the Pearl River Delta and the Bohai Rim. The integration process, which is determined by various factors, demonstrates that integration of infrastructure is the easiest to implement while the integration of industrial structure is the most difficult to coordinate.[36] The goal of regional coordinated development of the Yangtze River Delta is to pursue balanced social development in the unbalanced economic growth, promote the institutional innovation of the coordinated development of this region, and achieve the coordinated development of the economy, society and environment in this region.[37] As a region with great development potential after the Pearl River Delta and the Yangtze River Delta, the Beijing-Tianjin-Hebei region has recently become the focus of scholars. The Beijing-Tianjin-Hebei metropolitan area is one of China's most economically developed regions and also the political and cultural center. It is also an important supporting area for China's participation in international competition and modernization. Accelerating the integration of the Beijing-Tianjin-Hebei metropolitan area meets not only the development needs of Beijing, Tianjin, and Hebei but also the strategic needs to promote China's active participation in international competition and regional coordinated development.[38] Scholars have conducted some preliminary research on various aspects of Beijing-Tianjin-Hebei metropolitan governance, including the difficulties and problems, the metropolitan governance model and coordinated development mechanism, the interaction of government and enterprise (public), the development direction of regional industrial under the new orientation of the urban function, the division of labor and cooperation mechanism, the establishment of the metropolitan governance model, the governance coordination mechanism and policies.[39]

In addition to the above three regions, the development of other metropolitan areas in China has also received attention. For example, on the analysis of the urban agglomeration model of Changsha, Zhuzhou and Xiangtan, some scholars put forward the spatial organization model of the integration of this metropolitan area and the corresponding policies.[40] They also proposes a network government cooperation model based on the construction of government environment, economic environment, ecological environment and information environment, with particular emphasis on restricting government's breach of contract and non-cooperation from the perspective of system design, so as to reduce the risk of default and non-cooperation between inter-provincial governments and effectively achieve the cooperation of the public affairs in Changsha, Zhuzhou and Xiangtan urban agglomeration.[41] Some scholars have also proposed that the construction of the Changsha-Zhuzhou-Xiangtan urban agglomeration experimental area is a major strategic measure for China to promote the rise of the central region and the coordinated development of the eastern, central and western regions in the new development stage. Combined with the actual situation of the region, they also put forward the important premises, basic principles and major programs for the establishment of the management organization of this area.[42] Further research on the Changsha-Zhuzhou-Xiangtan urban agglomeration also focused on the necessary conditions for the construction of a resource-conserving and environment-friendly society, the promotion of the economic development and the improvement of the social comprehensive service function of the Changsha-Zhuzhou-Xiangtan urban agglomeration.[43] Besides, from the perspective of regional public management, some scholars analyzed the various non-cooperative dilemmas and corresponding causes in the development of Shandong Peninsula urban agglomeration, suggesting that the cooperation of urban agglomeration should focus on the solution of regional public problems and the promotion of regional public interests to pursue the construction of equal cooperation mechanism on the basis of mutual benefit. As a result, abandoning the stereotype which relied solely on the idea of administrative power division and administrative district change, building an organizational platform and collaborative mechanism for urban agglomeration cooperation with the concept of compound administration.[44]

The research on collaborative governance of these metropolitan areas provides an important research basis for analyzing the holistic collaborative governance model of local governments in China's metropolitan area. However, at present, Chinese scholars have not systematically and deeply analyzed and constructed the specific mechanism of metropolitan collaborative management from the perspective of holistic governance, which is exactly one of the tasks this research has attempted to accomplish.

## The governance theory of metropolitan area based on complex network governance

The metropolitan governance theory led by the complex network governance incorporates local governments, non-profit organizations and the private sector in the region into the category of network governance. By combining these regional governance subjects through various linkages, this theory emphasizes the achievement of common objective through cooperation and coordination between various governance subjects.

American scholars Stephen Goldsmith and William Eggers believe that the era of hierarchical government management is facing an end and will be replaced by a completely different model, which is called the network governance. Network management represents the convergence of four influential trends in the world that change the shape of the public sector (see Figure 2.2), namely third-party government, collaborative government, digital revolution and consumer demand. Network governance:

> represents the synthesis of these four trends, combining the high level of public-private collaboration characteristic of third-party government with the robust network management capabilities of joined-up government, and then using technology to connect the network together and give citizens more choices in service delivery options.[45]

Network governance includes a high degree of public-private partnerships and government's management capabilities over network.

When the government relies less on public employees and more on cooperative networks and contractors for public affairs, the ability of

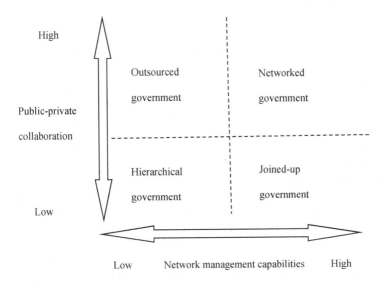

*Figure 2.2* Network governance.

Source: Stephen Goldsmith and William D. Eggers, *Governing by Network: The New Shape of the Public Sector* (Washington, DC: Brookings Institution Press, 2004), 20.

government agencies to manage the network is as much as the ability to manage their own public employees, determining the success or failure of the organization.[46]

The Institutional Collective Action Framework (ICA) is one of the theories of the complex governance network paradigm. In regional governance, the ICA theory, which was originally used to explain individual behavior, can institutionally define individual actors in regional cooperation, such as local governments or government departments and their constituencies. Institutional collective action clearly focuses on the externalities of choice in the fragmentation system. Richard Feiock and others advocated the application of the ICA to analyze collaborative governance among local governments. He proposed that in this system, decisions made by an independent and formal government agency would not take into account the costs or benefits that these decisions would bring to voters in the constituency, nor would they take into account the influences of the policy outcomes over other government departments. For example, uncoordinated investments between local governments can result in over-production and over-service delivery; the rules of one government department can undermine the effectiveness of other subjects; an organization's projects compete with, rather than complement, projects from other organizations. Therefore, ICA is concerned with higher levels of collective action issues in government departments, such as public goods, natural monopolies, economies of scale and management of public pond resources. This framework focuses on and compares the impact of alternative mechanisms that mitigate the adverse consequences of these decision-making externalities.[47] Some scholars have analyzed the game behaviors in the cooperation of local governments in urban agglomerations, and discussed the urban cooperation models such as guaranteed games, repeated prisoner's dilemma game and bargaining game.[48]

Social networks also play an important role in regional local government cooperation. As individuals in social networks, the local governments' opportunities and constraints in the region are shaped by the social-structure environment. This is due to the fact that the number, type and degree of overlap between local governments and other members of the region will be bring different levels of social capital gains. Kelly LeRoux and others believe that social networks play an important role in regional local government cooperation. After studying the degree of influence of multiple complex networks in the metropolitan area on intergovernmental collaboration, they proposed that it will be easier to form intergovernmental connections (such as the signing of an intergovernmental contract) if local government officials who representing their respective jurisdictions could participate in local intergovernmental cooperation organizations (such as metropolitan area committees) or hold the same professional background (such as with an MPA degree).[49]

In the field of public policy analysis, Peter de Leon and others proposed a collaborative policy network research framework in regional governance.[50] They believe that there are seven structural characteristics in a cooperative policy network: The first is representativeness or diversity. The representation, diversity or heterogeneity of stakeholders is more conducive to the formation of cooperation, and the homogeneity of participants does not necessarily lead to collaboration. As long as stakeholders are interested in the content of the collaboration and they have diverse characteristics, it is possible to achieve collaboration. The second is reciprocity. The reciprocity of partnerships is one of the important factors in achieving cooperation between members of the policy network. Each participant does not only want to gain revenue from the cooperative network, but more importantly, they want to better achieve common goals through cooperation. The third is the horizontal power structure. The greater the degree of decentralization in the cooperative network, the more equal exchange and interaction between members, thereby increasing their willingness to support cooperation. The fourth is embeddedness. Embedded theory argues that people make choices based on past collaborative experiences and are particularly inclined to build interactions with members they trust. Trading behavior is deeply embedded in social networks, and the trust generated by the interaction between people helps to prevent illegal behavior. Cooperative contracts are more common in the public sector than in the private sector, so a large number of trading behaviors arise from the original and trusted collaborators. In a cooperative policy network, it is still uncertain whether embeddedness will change over time in the context of formal or informal relationships, thus creating multiple and overlapping relationships. However, if this is true, it will illustrate how a collaborative policy network can produce spill-over effects on other policies. In this sense, embedding can be seen as "diversity," that is, the emergence of multiple relationships of members in a policy network, which is used to determine how the existence of multidimensional relationships affects the possibility of embedding, trust and future network development. The fifth is the formal degree of trust and relationship. Network relationships can be expressed in varying degrees of relationship, from formal contracts, regulatory guidelines, procedural steps to informal exchanges. The formality of network relationships can affect the degree of trust in a collaborative relationship network. Some scholars believe that with the development of trust among network participants, the formality of the relationship between them will decline, leading that "familiarity has fostered trust." In contrast, some scholars believe that it is the formal cooperation which can maintain a permanent cooperation. Although formal relations will remain relatively stable from the beginning, this does not rule out the role of informal relationships in network relationships. In a cooperative network relationship, it still needs to be further investigated that whether more formal contracts be used, and whether the interactions of collaborators in different departments will fluctuate as the formality of their relationship fluctuate. Of course, the trust between members in a cooperative network relationship is based on their reliability, mission consistency and transparent communication and interaction. The sixth is participatory decision-making. Participatory decision-making is an important part of participatory democracy and represents the interests and needs of all multistakeholders related to policy issues. This process requires greater transparency and fairness. In a cooperative policy network, the requirements for transparency and fairness can be reflected by the relationship of perceptions between policy network members with decision-making power and other network members toward whether or not the decision makers are transparent and fair. That is the also known as cognitive social structure, which provides information about how each network member perceives other members, that is, how the network members establish relationships with other members. The seventh is cooperative leadership. In a collaborative policy network, leadership positions are often shared by stakeholders and sometimes rotated among stakeholders. In some cases, a very centralized leadership structure is formed, while in some cases a wide variety of leadership positions are formed. In a cooperative policy network, leaders should represent fairness, and leadership should be performed by similar members of the network. Leadership is chosen not because they have the greatest financial impact or have the most legitimacy, but because of their connections to similar numbers and types of stakeholders in the network. Therefore, those "structurally equivalent" stakeholders, that is, those with similar or equal number relationships with other members, will occupy the position of the leader in the network.

For this new research field, after summarizing relevant researches, Chinese scholars pointed out that as a new governance model, network governance has formed two schools, that is, actor-centered institutionalism and complex networks management. Network governance is committed to the realization of interactions and mutually beneficial cooperation between stakeholders. And the key mechanisms of network governance are trust mechanism, value coordination and information sharing coordination mechanism.[51] Some scholars believe that the network governance can promote the socialization and flattening of government governance, which is conducive to the transformation of government functions and the promotion of integration of public services.[52] Some scholars have defined network governance as:

> synergistic actions, with the purpose of optimizing public interests, taken by local governments cooperating with other non-government departments (including corporate organizations, social organizations, citizens, etc.) through ways of administrative authorization and purchasing of services under certain frameworks and contractual provisions.[53]

With the development of research, scholars have begun to apply network governance to the study of the metropolitan area. They believe that the networked governance model not only challenges and reflects on the governance model of the urban agglomeration dominated by governments and market, but also provides a new perspective concerning the problems of management system and relationship between urban governments that arise during the development of urban agglomerations. The current network governance relationship is gradually formed within the scope of China's urban agglomerations. "The member cities and their functional departments have formed an all-round, multi-level comprehensive network governance relationship with market organizations and social organizations."[54] Of course, this network governance model is still in the early stage of development, and it is necessary to improve the network supervision and performance evaluation mechanism.

Recently, discussions on the application of network governance mechanisms in river basin governance have become more prominent. Some scholars believe that because the network governance mechanism is more flexible than the bureaucratic mechanism, more stable than the market mechanism and more applicable than the autonomous mechanism, the evolution from the bureaucratic mechanism to the network mechanism is the choice of path toward the innovation of the river basin governance mechanism in China. The basic framework of the mechanism is the organic combination of multi-level governance of central-local governments and government-enterprise partnership governance.[55] In environmental governance, the government and enterprises form a partnership governance mechanism through public voluntary schemes, unilateral agreements and negotiation agreements. This partnership governance mechanism is an important supplement to the bureaucratic system and market mechanism in environmental governance. Therefore, local governments should actively implement incentive policies, strengthen corporate social responsibility and promote voluntary environmental actions of enterprises at different levels.[56] On the basis of the intergovernmental relationship theory, scholars propose to establish a cooperation mechanism led by the regional management organization, that is, to establish a management system which is characterized by clear relationship, equal consultation and division of responsibility between the river basin management institutions, local governments and national functional departments.[57] In addition, in the process of cross-domain public crisis governance, some scholars pointed out that due to the "off domain" public crisis, the regional social operation mechanism will be interrupted. Therefore, the "network-based" regional public management system is used as a platform to integrate vertical and horizontal resources within government system and gather market and social resources outside the government system, thus achieving effective governance of the "off domain" public crisis.[58]

Therefore, the metropolitan governance paradigm led by the complex governance network carries out the research on the cooperative governance of the metropolitan area from the perspective of complex networks. The network governance mechanism formed by this is one of the important sources of literatures for analyzing the overall cooperative governance mechanism of the metropolitan area.

## The theory of intergovernmental collaboration based on holistic governance

As a new approach of governance after the new public management, the application of holistic governance in regional collaborative governance is an emerging research field of public management. Holistic governance is a return of Holism.[59] "Holism" is a view opposite to "individualism." It comes from the elaboration of sociological research methods by the French social thinker Émile Durkheim in the nineteenth century. Since the twentieth century, the holistic model adopted by holism has gradually become an important method widely used in social science research. In the twenty-first century, the holistic view has regained attention due to the increasingly serious "fragmentation" of the public sphere caused by new public management. Perri 6, a British scholar, proposed the concept of holistic governance in 2002.[60]

The study of holistic governance in countries outside China has experienced the development process from "holistic government" to "holistic governance." As far as the "holistic government" is concerned, it is aimed at solving the administrative barriers that exist in the provision of public services by various government departments, emphasizing the establishment of horizontal integration and linkages between different government departments and their functions. Scholars such as Perri 6 and Christopher Pollitt have conducted in-depth research on the integration of government functions, the synergy of government actions and the integrity of government-provided public services.[61] At the same time, some developed countries have also set off a wave of practice of "holistic government" reform. With the development of network and information technology and the increasingly serious "fragmentation" of the public sector, Perri 6 put forward the "holistic governance" theory.[62] This theory is characterized by collaboration, integration and "transboundary," focusing on the overall interests. It also emphasizes that the government must not only integrate the institutions and functions of various departments within the government when conducting public affairs governance, but also promote the collaboration between governments, private sectors and non-profit organizations to form a holistic governance network. In addition, Patrick Dunleavy, a British scholar, also pointed out that the governance of the digital age should focus on the reintegration of public services, emphasizing the holistic and coordinated decision-making approach.[63]

Perri 6 believes that there are three aspects needed to be integrated for government in holistic governance (see Figure 2.3). One is the integration of different or the same levels of governance. For example, the integration between local government departments, between the central government and local government departments or between officials of one country's local trade standards bureau and national trade standards bureau, or even

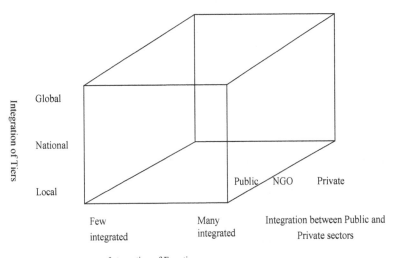

*Figure 2.3* Holistic governance.

Source: Perri 6, *Governing in the Round: Strategies for Holistic Government*, London: Demos, 1999, 29.

with personnel of global trade standards institutions or national environmental or information protection organizations at the global level. The
second is function integration. That is to say, the integration of the internal
functions of the government, which can be the integration of the functions
of a government agency, or the integration of multiple functional agencies.
For example, only the integration within the health and social security
sectors, or multiple sectors involved in the integration for the reconstruc-
tion of the city. Third, the integration between the public and private
sectors. In order to provide better services, the public sector will establish
cooperation with non-profit organizations and the private sector in the form
of contract outsourcing, administrative corporatization and privatization.

Therefore, holistic governance emphasizes the integration of three
aspects. One is the integration of different levels of government and the
same level of government. The second is the integration of the functions of
various government departments. The third is the integration of the public
sector with the private sector and non-profit organizations. As the holistic
governance theory is characterized by collaboration, integration and
"transboundary," it emphasizes cross-sectoral collaboration in regional
governance, focusing on the formation of collaborative mechanisms
between governments and other social subjects in the region. The overall
interests play an important role in the coordinated governance of local
governments in the metropolitan area.

The research on holistic governance in China is still in a preliminary
stage. There are several important concepts related to holistic governance,
including Holistic Government, Joined-up Government and Cross-agency
Collaboration, etc. Chinese scholarship mainly focuses on the theory and
methods of Western holistic governance, and conducts research on internal
coordination and cross-departmental collaboration among government
departments.[64] At present, the application of holistic governance theory in
regional governance is an emerging research field of public management.
Some scholars in Taiwan have translated "holistic governance" into "all-
dimensional governance" and believe that the realm of all-dimensional
governance must be based on three main strategies, including a dense and
detailed information system, an organizational system and a personnel
administration system.[65] The holistic governance reflects the cross-regional
characteristics. The growth of the North American Free Trade Area and
the European Union indicates the trend that governance must take into
account cross-regional and global public governance. Some scholars in
China believe that while holistic governance focuses on the internal
coordination mechanism of the government, it should try to establish an
intergovernmental consultation platform and a regional cooperation mechanism, and build a governance network between the government and other

social subjects, such as non-governmental organizations and private sectors, to jointly manage social public affairs.[66]

It is worth mentioning that several scholars in China have analyzed the similarities and differences between holistic governance and network governance. They pointed out that, in following the new public management theory, both holistic governance and network governance are attempting to make further amendments and development. The two theories are the same in terms of operational mechanism, emphasizing the realization of cooperation and co-governance between the government and other social entities on public affairs, and responding more quickly and efficiently to the needs of the public. They are also consistent in the pursuit of the goal effect. They all emphasize to improve the performance of the government by endowing the internal executive bodies with certain autonomy, and avoid excessive decentralization and inefficient coordination. Both pursue the goal of improving public services, advocating the promotion of marketization and privatization of public services while insisting on the quality and public welfare of public services.[67] Thus, they depend on each other and promote each other. However, holistic governance and network governance are different in theoretical origins. The theory and methodological basis of holistic governance is holism and new public service theory, so it is a new "Durkheim path." While network governance theory is a variety of specific governance models based on the theory of institutional economics, self-organization, governance and corporate network governance.[68] And the focus of the two theories is not the same. The theory of holistic governance mainly emphasizes "self-cultivation," emphasizing effective improvement and governance of "fragmentation" within government departments, thus enabling harmonized and efficient operation between different levels of government and government department. Network governance pays more attention to "external connection" and the scope of its research is broader. It not only pays attention to the performance of governance networks formed by various interest groups within the government, but also emphasizes the benign interaction between government, market and society, highlighting the governance network of public services.[69]

Some scholars have begun to interpret the trend of governance and future models of metropolitan areas in China from a new perspective of holistic governance. For example, some scholars have proposed that as an important form of government collaborative governance, holistic governance plays an important role in regional collaborative governance. Therefore, efforts must be strengthened in the holistic governance model, coordination mechanism, trust mechanism and monitoring mechanism.[70] Some scholars believe that the frequent occurrence of cross-border pollution events reflects the contradiction between the pollution control mode of a single administrative region and the external characteristics of environmental pollution. The problems of environmental pollution cannot be solved independently by a single local government, so it is necessary to establish an effective cross-regional and inter-basin governance mechanisms and local government cooperation mechanisms to address cross-border environmental issues.[71] What's more, some scholars believe that the coordination and integration of local governments advocated by the theory of holistic governance has become an important way to promote governance of cross-border public affairs in metropolitan areas. The holistic governance model of cross-border public affairs of metropolitan local governments, composed of cross-regional cooperative organizations, local governments, non-governmental organizations and the private sector, is of great significance to achieve effective governance of cross-border public affairs in Beijing-Tianjin-Hebei metropolitan area.[72]

In summary, the existing literature has involved the introduction and research of local government collaboration in different levels and perspectives, and formed a preliminary research framework, which has the practical significance and academic value. However, these documents have not yet conducted systematic research on the government-led collaborative governance model which is composed of governments, private departments and NGOs in the metropolitan area, from the perspective of holistic governance, which is exactly what the local government in the current metropolitan area needs when solving regional coordination problems. In addition, for the cooperation model of local governments in the current metropolitan area in China, the construction of the holistic cooperative organization and collaborative governance mechanism in the region is particularly important, while the analysis and research in this aspect have yet to be deepened and detailed. Therefore, this study takes the theory proposed by the "metropolitan governance paradigm dominated by regional multi-party cooperation" as an important research basis, and take the governance mechanism formed by the "metropolitan governance paradigm dominated by complex governance network" as an important resource of literature. Based on the above, this study focuses on analyzing, responding to and solving the problems of local government's cross-border public affairs collaboration from the perspective of "holistic governance," and studies the operation of the holistic cooperative governance mechanism of the local government in the metropolitan area and the construction of the holistic collaborative organization, exploring the model of holistic collaborative governance in the metropolitan area that is adapted to inclusive development.

# Conclusion

Based on the analysis and review of the governance theory of intergovernment cooperation in the metropolitan area, this chapter points out that with the development of regional governance practice, the theory of collaborative governance in the metropolitan area has also flourished. As a result, three important theories are formed gradually, that is, the theory of metropolitan governance based on regional multi-subject cooperation, the theory of metropolitan governance based on complex governance networks and the theory of intergovernmental collaboration led by holistic governance theory.

The theory of metropolitan governance based on regional multi-party cooperation tries to find a balance between the "government model" dominated by "state intervention" and the "multi-center governance model" dominated by "market," advocating to form a collaborative mechanism between different levels of government, social groups and the private sectors in the metropolitan area to jointly solve regional public affairs. The theory of metropolitan governance based on the complexity governance network incorporates the government, the private sector and the third sector in the region into the scope of network governance subjects, emphasizing the benign interaction between government, market and society, and advocating the achievement of common network goal through cooperation and coordination among organizations. The theory of holistic governance advocates cross-sectoral collaboration in regional governance and focuses on the formation of collaborative mechanisms between governments and other social subjects in the region. It emphasizes that the government should not only integrate the institutions and functions of various departments within the government, but also promote cooperation between the governments, the private sectors and non-profit organizations, thus forming a holistic governance network. Therefore, the theory of holistic governance is of great significance for solving the problem of local government collaboration in the governance of metropolitan areas.

This study is based on the theory of metropolitan governance based on regional multi-party cooperation and the theory of metropolitan governance based on complex governance networks, focusing on analyzing, responding to and solving the problems in the process of local government's cross-border public affairs cooperation in the metropolitan area from the perspective of "Holistic Governance" theory, then constructing the theoretical framework of the holistic cooperative governance of local governments in the metropolitan area. The framework analyzes various mechanisms, including trust mechanism, communication mechanism, interest coordination and compensation mechanism, monitoring and

48 *Intergovernmental collaborative governance*

evaluation mechanism from perspectives of the upper-level government (central government or provincial government), metropolitan local government, cross-regional cooperative organization, private sector, non-profit organization, etc. Based on the holistic collaborative governance mechanism, this study also explores the collaborative governance model of metropolitan area which is composed of the central government, the local governments of the metropolitan area, cross regional integrated cooperative organizations, non-profit organizations and the private sector.

## Notes

1 Robert L. Bish and Vincent Ostrom, *Understanding Urban Government: Metropolitan Reform Reconsidered*, (Washington, D.C.: American Enterprise Institute, 1973).
2 David Osborne and Ted Gaebler, *Reinventing Government: How the Entrepreneurial Spirit Is Transforming the Public Sector*, (Reading, MA: Addison-Wesley, 1992).
3 Richard Feiock, *Metropolitan Governance: Conflict, Competition, and Cooperation*, (Washington, D.C.: Georgetown University Press, 2004), 7.
4 Allan D. Wallis, "The Third Wave: Current Trends in Regional Governance," *National Civic Review*, Vol. 83, No. 3, Summer–Fall 1994; Allan D. Wallis, "Inventing Regionalism: A Two-phase Approach," *National Civic Review*, Vol. 83, No. 3, Fall–Winter 1994.
5 H. V. Savitch and R. Vogel, *Regional Politics: American in A Post-City Age*, (London: Sage Publications, 1996), pp. 110, 112; H. V. Savitch and R. Vogel, "Paths to New Regionalism," *State and Local Government Review*, Vol. 32, No. 3, 2000; H. V. Savitch, "Territory and Power: Rescaling for a Global Era," *Proceedings of the International Conference on Urban and Regional Development in the 21st Century*, (Sun Yat-sen University, December 17–18, 2011).
6 H. V. Savitch, "Territory and Power: Rescaling for a Global Era," *Proceedings of the International Conference on Urban and Regional Development in the 21st Century*, (Sun Yat-sen University, December 17–18, 2011).
7 See Wang Xu, Luo Sidong, *Local Government in the New Urbanization Period of the United States: The Game Between Regional Coordination and Local Autonomy*, (Xiamen University Press, 2010), 43–45.
8 Vincent, Ostrom, Robert, L. Bish and Elinor, Ostrom, *Local Government in the United States*, (San Francisco: ICS Press), 72–80.
9 H. V. Savitch, "Territory and Power: Rescaling for a Global Era," *Proceedings of the International Conference on Urban and Regional Development in the 21st Century*, (Sun Yat-sen University, December 17–18, 2011).
10 Cui Jing. "Dadushiqu kuajiegonggongshiwu yunxingmoshi: fujixiezuo yu zhenghe" ["The Operational Mode of Metropolitan Cross-jurisdiction Public Affairs: the Cooperation and Integration Between Government"]. *Gaige* [*Reform*] vol. 7 (2011), 82–87.
11 Ye Lin, "Xinquyuzhuyi de xingqiyufazhan: yigezongshu" ["A Review of Literature on New Regionalism"]. *Gonggongxingzhengpinglun* [*Journal of Public Administration*] vol. 3 (2010), 175–190.

12 H. V. Savitch, R. Vogel, "Paths to New Regionalism," *State and Local Government Review*, Vol. 32, No. 3 (2000).
13 H. V. Savitch, "Territory and Power: Rescaling for a Global Era," *Proceedings of the International Conference on Urban and Regional Development in the 21st Century*, (Sun Yat-sen University, December 17–18, 2011).
14 H. V. Savitch, R. Vogel, Ye Lin, "Beyond the Rhetoric: Lessons from Louisville's Consolidation," *American Review of Public Administration*, Vol. 40, No. 1 (2010).
15 See Lin Shangli, *Guoneizhengfujianguanxi* [*Domestic Intergovernmental Relations*] (Hangzhou: Zhejiang renmin chubanshe [Zhejiang People's Publishing house], 1998); Xie Qinkui, "Zhongguo zhengfu de fujiguanxi yanjiu" ["Intergovernmental Relations in China"]. *Beijing daxuexuebao (zhexueshehuikexue ban)* [*Journal of Peking University (Humanities And Social Science)*] vol. 37, No. 197 (2000), 26–34; Bo Guili, *Jiquan fenquan yu guojia de xingshuai* [*Centralization and Decentralization and the Rise and Fall of the Country*] (Beijing: jingjikexuechubanshe [Economic Science Press], 2001).
16 See Chen Ruilian, Yang Aiping. "Cong quyugonggongguanlidaoquyuzhiliyanjiu: lishi de zhuanxing" ["The Historical Transformation from Regional Public Management to Regional Governance"], *Nankaixuebao (zhexueshehuikexue ban)* [*Nankai Journal (Philosophy, Literature and Social Science Edition)*] vol. 2 (2012), 48–57; Chen Ruilian, *Quyugonggongguanlililunyushijianyanjiu* [*Research on Theory and Practice of Regional Public Management*] (Beijing: Zhongguo shehuikexue chubanshe [Chinese Social Science Press], 2008); Chen Ruilian. "Lun quyu gonggongguanli yanjiu de yuanqi yu fazhan" ["Research on the Origin and Development of Regional Public Management"]. *Zhengzhixueyanjiu* [*Cass Journal of Political Science*] vol. 4 (2003), pp. 75–84; Chen Ruilian, Kong Kai, "Zhongguoquyugonggongguanliyanjiu de fazhanyuqianzhan" ["Development and Prospect of Regional Public Management Research in China"]. *Xueshuyanjiu* [*Academic Research*] vol. 5 (2009), 45–49.
17 Yang Aiping, Chen Ruilian, "Cong 'Xingzhengquxingzhengdaoquyugonggongguanli'-zhengfuzhilixingtaishanbian de yizhongbijiaofenxi" ["From Administrative District Administration to Regional Public Management: A Comparative Analysis of the Evolution of Government Governance"]. *Jiangxi shehuikexue* [*Jiangxi Social Sciences*] vol. 11 (2004), 23–31.
18 Liu Junde, "Lunzhonguodaludadushiquxingzhengzuzhiyuguanlimoshichuangxin-jianlunzhujiangsanjiaozhou de zhengqugaige" ["Study on the innovation of the administrative organization and management of the metropolitan areas in Chinese mainland: A case study on the administrative innovation of the pearl river delta"]. *Jingjidili* [*Economic Geography*] vol. 21, No. 2 (March 2001), 201–207.
19 Wang Jian, Bao Jing, Liu Xiaokang, Wang Dianli, "'Fuhexingzheng' de tichu—jiejuedangdaizhongguoquyujingjiyitihuayuxingzhengquhuachongtu de xinsilu" ["Proposal of Combined Administration: A new way to Solve the Conflicts between Regional Economic Integration and Administrative Divisions in Contemporary China"]. *Zhongguoxingzhengguanli* [*Chinese Public Administration*] vol. 3 (2004), 44–48.
20 Zhang Jingen, "Xinquyuzhuyi: meiguodadushiquzhili de xinsilu" ["New Regionalism: New Ideas for the Management of American Metropolitan Areas"]. *Zhongshandaxuexuebao* [*Journal of Sun Yat-sen University* (social science edition)] vol. 50, No. 1 (2010), 131–141.

21 Ye lin, "Zhaohuizhengfu: 'hougonggongguanli' shiyuxia de quyuzhilitansuo" ["Retrieving the Government: Exploring Regional Governance from the Perspective of Post-New Public Management"]. *Xueshuyanjiu* [*Academic Research*] vol. 5 (2012), 64–69.

22 Chen Shengyong, Ma Bin, "Quyujianzhengfuhezuo: quyujingjiyitihua de lujingxuanze" ["Inter-regional government cooperation: the path choice of regional economic integration"]. *Zhengzhixueyanjiu* [*Cass Journal of Political Science*] vol. 1 (2004), 24–34.

23 See Zhou Li-an, "Jinshengboyizhongzhengfuguanyuan de jiliyuhezuo—jianlunwoguo defang baohuzhuyi he chongfujianshewentichangqicunzai de yuanyin" ["The Incentive and Cooperation of Government Officials in the Political Tournaments: An Interpretation of the Prolonged Local Protectionism and Duplicative Investments in China"]. *Jingjiyanjiu* [Economic Research Journal] vol. 6 (2004), 33–40; Zhou Li-an, "Zhongguo difang guanyuan de jinshengjinbiaosaimoshiyanjiu" ["Governing China's Local Officials: An Analysis of Promotion Tournament Model"]. *Jingjiyanjiu* [*Economic Research Journal*] vol. 7 (2007), 36–50; Zhou Li-an, *Zhuanxingzhong de difangzhengfu: guanyuan de jiliyuzhili* [*Local Government in Transition: Official Incentives and Governance*] (Shanghai People's Press, 2008); Zhou Li-an, "Guanyuan jinsheng jingzheng yu bianjiexiaoying: yi shengqujiaojie didai de jingjifazhan weili" ["Official promotion competition and border effect: taking the economic development of the provincial border area as an example"]. *Jinrong yanjiu* [*Journal of Financial Research*] vol. 3 (2011), 15–26; Zhang Keyun, *Quyu dazhan yu quyu jingji de guanxi* [*Regional war and regional economic relations*] (Beijing: Democracy and Construction Press, 2001); Feng Xingyuan, "Lunxiaquzhengfujian de zhidujingzheng" ["System Competition among Jurisdictional Governments"]. *Guojia Xingzheng xueyuan xuebao* [*Journal of National School of Administration*], vol. 6 (2001), 27–32.

24 Liu Yaping, *Dangdai zhongguo difangzhengfujian jingzheng* [*Competition among local governments in contemporary China*] (Beijing: Shehuikexuewenxianchubanshe [Beijing: Social Science Literature Publishing House], 2007).

25 Jin Taijun, "Cong xingzhengquxingzhengdaoquyugonggongguanli—zhengfuzhilixingtaishanbian de boyifenxi" ["From administering administrative divisions to regional public administration: a game analysis of evolution in the pattern of governance by the government"]. *Zhongguoshehuikexue* [*Social Sciences in China*] vol. XXIX, No. 4 (November 2008), 48–62.

26 See Yang Long, Peng Yanqiang, "Lijiezhongguo difangzhengfuhezuo—xingzhengguanxiaquanrangdu de shijiao" ["Understanding Chinese local government cooperation—The perspective of the transfer of administrative jurisdiction"]. *Zhengzhixueyanjiu* [*Cass Journal of Political Science*] vol. 4 (2009), 61–66; Yang Long, Zheng Chunyong, "Difanghezuo dui zhengfujianguanxi de tuozhan" ["Local cooperation to expand intergovernmental relations"]. *Tansuoyuzhengming* [*Exploration and Free Views*] vol. 1 (2011), 38–41.

27 Zhang Jingen, "Cong quyuxingzhengdaoquyuzhili: dangdaizhongguoquyujingjiyitihua de fazhanluxiang" ["On the Development Rout of Current China's Regional Economy Unity: from Regional Administration to a Region Governed"]. *Xueshuyanjiu* [*Academic Research*] vol. 9 (2009), 42–49.

28 Yang Aiping, "Lunquyuyitihuaxiade quyuzhengfujianhezuo: dongyin, moshijizhanwang" ["On Interregional Government Cooperation under Regional

Integration—Motivation, model and outlook"]. *Zhengzhixue yanjiu* [*Cass Journal of Political Science*] vol. 3 (2007), 77–86.

29 Yang Aiping, "Quyuhezuozhong de fujiqiyue: gainianyufenlei" ["A Research on Intergovernmental Agreement for Regional Cooperation: Concept and Classification"]. *Zhongguoxingzhengguanli* [*Chinese Public Administration*] vol. 6 (2011), 100–104.

30 See Yang Aiping, "Cong chuizhijilidaopingxingjili: defang zhengfuhezuo de liyijilijizhichuangxin" ["From Vertical Incentive to Horizontal Incentive: As an Innovation of Benefit Encouragement Mechanism in Local Government Cooperation"]. *Xueshuyanjiu* [*Academic Research*] vol. 5 (2011), 47–53; Liu Yaping, Liu Linlin, "Zhongguoquyuzhengfuhezuo de kunjingyuzhanwang" ["Predicament and Prospect of the Cooperation among China's Local Governments"], *Xueshuyanjiu* [*Academic Research*] vol. 12 (2012), 38–45; Yang Aiping, "Cong zhengzhidongyuandaozhidujianshe: zhusanjiaoyitihuazhongde zhengfuchuangxin" ["From Political Mobilization to Institutional Construction: Government Innovation in Pearl River Delta's Integration"]. *Huanan shifandaxuexuebao (shehuikexue ban)* [*Journal of South China Normal University (Social Science Edition)*] vol. 6 (2011), 114–120.

31 Liu Yaping, Liu Linlin, "Zhongguo quyu zhengfu hezuo de kunjing yu zhanwang" ["Predicament and Prospect of the Cooperation among China's Local Governments"]. *Xueshuyanjiu* [*Academic Research*] vol. 12 (2012), 38–45.

32 Chen Ruilian, Liu Yaping, "Fan zhusanjiaoquyuzhengfu de hezuoyuchuangxin" ["Cooperation and Innovation of the Pan-Pearl River Delta Regional Government"]. *Xueshuyanjiu* [*Academic Research*] vol. 1 (2007), 42–50.

33 Zhang Jingen, "Quyu gonggongguanli zhidu chuangxin fenxi" ["Analysis of regional public management system innovation: Taking the Pearl River Delta as an example"]. *Zhengzhixueyanjiu* [*Cass Journal of Political Science*] vol. 3 (2010), 63–75; Zhang Jingen, "Shilun xinquyuzhuyi shiye xiade fanzhusanjiao quyu hezuo" ["On Regional Cooperation from View of New Regionalism in the Pan-Pearl River Delta"]. *Wuhan daxuexuebao* [*Wuhan University Journal (Philosophy & Social Sciences)*] vol. 61, No. 3 (May 2008), 351–357.

34 Feng Bangyan, Yin Laisheng, "Chengshi qunquyu zhili jiegou de dongtai yanbian: yi zhujiang sanjiaozhou weili" ["Dynamic Evolution of Urban Community Regional Governance Structure—Taking the Pearl River Delta as an example"]. *Chengshiwenti* [*Urban Problems*] vol. 7 (2011), 11–15.

35 Zhao Feng, Jiang Debo, "Changsanjiaoquyuhezuojizhi de jingyanyujinyibufazhansilu" ["Experience and Further Developing Route of the Cooperative Mechanism for Yangtze River Delta"]. *Zhongguoxingzhengguanli* [*Chinese Public Administration*] vol. 2 (2011), 81–84.

36 Zou Weixing, Zhou Liqun, "Quyujingjiyitihua jincheng pouxi: changsanjiao, zhusanjiaoyuhuanbohai" ["Analysis of Regional Economic Integration: Yangtze River Delta, Pearl River Delta and Bohai Rim Region"]. *Gaige* [*Reform*] vol. 10 (2010), 86–93.

37 See Chu Dajian, "Shanghai yu changsanjiao quyuxietiao fazhan zhongde wentisikao" ["Thinking on the Problems of the Coordinated Development Between Shanghai and Yangtze River Delta Region"]. *Shanghai chengshiguihua* [*Shanghai Urban Planning Review*] vol. 2 (2011), 7–9; Wang Fengyun, *Hexiegongjin zhongde zhengfu xietiao: changsanjiaochengshiqun de shizhengyanjiu* [*Government Coordination in Harmony and Progress: An Empirical Study*

of the Yangtze River Delta Urban Agglomeration] (Guangzhou: Zhongshan daxue chubanshe [Guangzhou: Sun Yat-sen University Press], 2009).

38  Zhu Erjuan, *"Shierwu" shiqijingjinjifazhanyanjiu (2009)* [*Study on Beijing-Tianjin-Hebei Development during the Twelfth Five-Year Plan Period (2009)*] (Beijing: Zhongguojingjichubanshe [Beijing: China Economic Publishing House], 2010).

39  Mu Aiying, Wu Jianqi, Wu Yiqing, *Jingjinji: Linian, moshiyujizhi* [*Beijing-Tianjin-Hebei: Ideas, Models and Mechanisms*] (Beijing: Zhongguo shehuikexue chubanshe [Beijing: Chinese Social Science Press], 2010).

40  Xie Shouhong, Ning Yuemin, "Dushuqu: Changzhutanyitihua de biyouzhilu" ["Metropolitan area: The only way of integration for Chang-Zhu-Tan area"]. *Jingjidili* [*Economic Geography*] vol. 25, No. 6 (November 2005), 834–837.

41  Fu Yongchao, Xu Xiaolin, "Fuji guanlililunyuchangzhutanchengshiqunzhengfuhezuojizhi" ["Intergovernmental Management Theory and Changsha-Zhuzhou-Xiangtan Governments Cooperation Mechanism"]. *Gonggongguanlixuebao* [*Journal of Public Management*] vol. 4, No. 2 (April 2007), 24–29.

42  Hunan Public Management Research Base, "Changzhutan shiyanqu guanlijigou shezhiyanjiu" ["Research on Establishment of Management Institutions in Chang-Zhu-Tan Pilot-area"]. *Zhongguoxingzhengguanli* [*Chinese Public Administration*] vol. 2 (2010), 85–88.

43  Luo Chuanling, "xinxihua yu changzhutan chengshiqun 'Liangxingshehui' jianshechutan" ["Research on information-based system and the resource-saving and environment-friendly in the Chang-Zhu-Tan city group"]. *Jingjidili* [*Economic Geography*] vol. 29, No. 3 (March 2009), 415–419.

44  See Wang Dianli, "Quyugonggongguanli de zhiduyujizhichuangxintanxi: yi Shandong bandaochengshiqunweili" ["Analysis on the Innovation of System and Mechanism of Regional Public Management—Taking Shandong Peninsula Urban Agglomeration as an Example"]. *Beijing xingzhengxueyuanxuebao* [*Journal of Beijing Administrative College*] vol. 5 (2009), 11–15; Wang Dianli, "Bandaochengshiqunfazhan dongli yuzhangai de xingzhengxuefenxi" ["Administrative Analysis of the Driving Forces and Obstacles of Peninsula City Group Development"]. *Dongyueluncong* [*Dongyue Tribune*] vol. 30, No. 5 (May 2009), 30–34.

45  Stephen Goldsmith and William D. Eggers, *Governing by Network: The New Shape of the Public Sector* (Washington, D.C.: Brookings Institution Press, 2004), 19.

46  Stephen Goldsmith and William D. Eggers, *Wangluohuazhili: Gonggongbumen de xinxingtai* [*Governing by Network: The New Shape of the Public Sector*] (Beijing: Beijing daxuechubanshe [Peking University Press], 2008), 21.

47  Richard C. Feiock and John T. Scholz, *Self-Organizing Federalism: Collaborative Mechanisms to Mitigate Institutional Collective Action Dilemmas* (New York: Cambridge University Press, 2010), 3–6.

48  Annette Steinacker, "Game-Theoretic Models of Metropolitan Cooperation," in Richard C. Feiock (ed.), *Metropolitan Governance: Conflict, Competition, and Cooperation* (Washington, D.C.: Georgetown University Press, 2004), 48–51.

49  Kelly LeRoux, Paul W. Brandenburger and Sanjay K. Pandey, "Interlocal Service Cooperation in U.S. Cities: A Social Network Explanation," *Public Administration Review*, Vol. 70, No. 2 (2010).

50  Peter de Leon and Danielle Varda, "Toward a Theory of Collaborative Policy Networks: Identifying Structural Tendencies," *The Policy Studies Journal*, Vol. 37, No. 1 (2009).

Intergovernmental collaborative governance 53

51 Yin Yifen, "Wangluozhili: Gonggongguanli de xinkuangjia" ["Network Governance: A New Framework of Public Administration"]. *Gonggongguanlixuebao* [*Journal of Public Management*] vol. 4, No. 1 (January 2007), 89–96.

52 Chu Dajian, LI Zhongzheng, "Wangluozhili shijiaoxia de gonggongfuwu zhenghe chutan" ["Probe into the Integration of Public Service from the Perspective of Network Governance"]. *Zhongguoxingzhengguanli* [*Chinese Public Administration*] vol. 8 (2007), 34–36.

53 Yao Yinliang, Liu Bo, Wang Yingluo, "Difangzhengfu wangluozhili yu hexieshehui goujian de liluntantao" ["The Network Governance of Local Government and The Construction of Harmonious Society"]. *Zhongguoxingzhengguanli* [*Chinese Public Administration*] vol. 11 (2009), 91–94.

54 Yu Gangqiang, CaiLihui, "Zhongguodushiqunwangluohuazhilimoshiyanjiu" ["Governance by Network: The New Trend of Governing Pattern of Urban Agglomeration in China"]. *Zhongguoxingzhengguanli* [*Chinese Public Administration*] vol. 6 (2011), 93–98.

55 Li Yuansheng, Hu Yi, "Cong kecengdaowangluo: liuyuzhilijizhichuangxin de lujingxuanze" ["From the bureaucracy to the network: Path Choice of Innovation in River Basin Governance Mechanism"]. *Fuzhou dangxiaoxuebao* [*Journal of the Party School of Fuzhou*] vol. 2 (2010), 35–39.

56 Hu Yi, "Huanjingbaohu Zhong zhengfuyuqiyehuobanzhilijizhi" ["Government and corporate partner governance mechanism in environmental protection"]. *Xingzhengluntan* [*Administrative Tribune*] vol. 4 (2008), 80–82.

57 Xing Hua, "Shuiziyuan guanlixiezuo jizhi guancha: Liuyu yu xingzhengquyu fengong" ["The Observation of the Cooperation Mechanism of Water Resources Management: the river basin and the Administrative Regional Division"]. *Gaige* [*Reform*] vol. 5 (2011), 68–73.

58 Shen Chengcheng, JinTaijun, "'Tuoyu' gonggongweiji zhili yu quyugonggongguanli tizhichuangxin" ["'Disembodying' Public Crisis Management and Innovation of Regional Public Administration System"]. *Jianghaixuekan* [*Jianghai Academic Journal*] No. 1 (2011), 107–112.

59 Li Ruichang, "Gonggongzhilizhuanxing: zhengtizhuyifuxing" ["Transformation of Public Governance: Holism's Renaissance"]. *Jiangsu xingzhengxueyuanxuebao* [*Journal of Jiangsu Administration Institute*] vol. 46, No. 4 (2009), 102–107.

60 Perri 6, Diana Leat, Kimberly Seltzer and Gerry Stoker, *Towards Holistic Governance: The New Reform Agenda* (New York: Palgrave, 2002).

61 See Perri 6, *Governing in the Round: Strategies for Holistic Government* (London: Demos, 1999); Christopher Pollitt, "Joined-up Government: A Survey," *Political Studies Review*, Vol. 1, No. 1 (2003).

62 Perri 6, Diana Leat, Kimberly Seltzer and Gerry Stoker, *Towards Holistic Governance: The New Reform Agenda* (New York: Palgrave, 2002).

63 See Patrick Dunleavy, Helen Margetts, Simon Bastow and Jane Tinkler, "New Public Management Is Dead: Long Live Digital-Era Governance," *Journal of Public Administration Research and Theory*, Vol. 16, No. 3 (2006); Patrick Dunleavy, Helen Margetts, Simon Bastow and Jane Tinkler, *Digital Era Governance: IT Corporations, the State, and E-Government* (Oxford University Press, 2006).

64 See Zhou Zhiren, Jiang Minjuan. "Zhengtizhengfuxiade zhengcexietong: Lilunyufadaguojia de dangdaishijian" ["Policy coordination under the overall government: Theory and contemporary practice in developed countries"].

*Guojiaxingzhengxueyuanxuebao* [*Journal of Chinese Academy of Governance*] vol. 6 (2010), 28–33; Zhu Qianwei, "Cong xingonggongguanlidaozhengtixingzhili" ["From New Public Management to Holistic Governance"]. *Zhongguoxingzhengguanli* [*Chinese Public Administration*] vol. 10 (2008), 52–58.

65  Peng Jinpeng, "Quanguanxingzhili: Lilunyuzhiduhuacelue" ["Holistic Governance: Theory and Institutionalization Strategies"]. *Zhengzhikexueluncong (Taiwan)* [*Political Science Review (Taiwan)*] vol. 23 (2005).

66  Liu Bo, Wang Lili, Yao Yinliang, "Zhengtixing zhili yu wangluozhili de bijiao yanjiu" ["A Comparative Study of Holistic Governance and Network Governance"]. *Jingji shehui tizhi bijiao* [*Comparative Economic & Social Systems*] vol. 5 (2011), 134–140.

67  Liu Bo, Wang Lili, Yao Yinliang, "Zhengtixingzhiliyuwangluozhili de bijiaoyanjiu" ["A Comparative Study of Holistic Governance and Network Governance"]. *Jingji shehui tizhi bijiao* [*Comparative Economic & Social Systems*] vol. 5 (2011), 134–140.

68  Yao Yinliang, Liu Bo, Wang Yingluo, "Wangluozhili lilun zai defang zhengfu gonggongguanli shijian zhongde yunyong jiqi dui xingzhengtizhi gaige de qishi" ["The Application of theory of network governance in the practice of local government public management and Its Enlightenment to the Reform of Administrative System"]. *Renwen zazhi* [*The Journal of Humanities*] vol. 1 (2010), 76–85.

69  Liu Bo, Wang Lili, Yao Yinliang, "Zhengtixingzhiliyuwangluozhili de bijiaoyanjiu" ["A Comparative Study of Holistic Governance and Network Governance"]. *Jingji shehui tizhi bijiao* [*Comparative Economic & Social Systems*] vol. 5 (2011), 134–140.

70  Gao Jianhua, "Quyu gonggongguanli shiyu xiade zhengtixing zhili: kuajie zhili de yige fenxi kuangjia" ["The Holistic Governance of Governments' Cooperation under the Regional Public Management Perspective: An Analysis Framework of Cross-border Governance"]. *Zhongguo xingzheng guanli* [*Chinese Public Administration*] vol. 11 (2010), 77–81.

71  Yang Yan, Sun Tao, "Kuaqu yu huanjing zhili yu difangzhengfu hezuo jizhi yanjiu" ["Study on the Mechanism of Local Government Cooperation in Interregional Environment Governance"]. *Zhongguo xingzheng guanli* [*Chinese Public Administration*] vol. 1 (2009), 66–69.

72  Cui Jing, "Quyu difangzhengfu kuajie gonggongshiwu zhengtixingzhili moshi yanjiu: yi jingjinji dushiquan weili" ["A Study on the Overall Governance Model of Regional Local Governments' Cross-border Public Affairs Taking the Beijing-Tianjin-Hebei Metropolitan Area as an Example"]. *Zhengzhixueyanjiu* [*CASS Journal of Political Science*] vol. 2 (2012), 91–97.

# 3 The holistic collaborative governance mode of local government in metropolitan area

The holistic collaborative governance model composed of higher-level governments, regional acting subjects and cross-jurisdiction holistic collaborative organizations is an important way to achieve coordinated regional development. This chapter analyzes how to construct the holistic collaborative governance model of the metropolitan area, which is composed of four parts: the integration of collaborative governance system and the construction of information platform, the construction of a cross-jurisdiction holistic collaborative organization, the establishment and improvement of a comprehensive collaborative governance mechanism, and the formation of a comprehensive collaborative governance network.

## The integration of collaborative governance system and the construction of information platform

The integration of internal institutions and functions implemented by various local governments in the metropolitan area in accordance with the principle of functional correspondence is a prerequisite for achieving holistic collaborative governance. In order to achieve holistic governance better, local governments in the metropolitan area need to promote the integration of internal institutions and functions in accordance with the principle of functional correspondence, thus forming a unified personnel administration, fiscal expenditure and information network system within the region. Such a system can ensure that local governments in the metropolitan area form a close and effective cooperation with other members' functional departments when solving public problems related to the ecological and river basins (see Figure 3.1). At present, local governments in various metropolitan areas in China have problems of overlapping functions and overlapping organizations in dealing with public affairs. In order to solve this problem, all local governments in the region need to form a unified personnel administration, fiscal expenditure and information

network system within the region, so as to effectively solve regional problems. For example, in terms of environmental protection, the environmental protection department of the cross-regional holistic collaborative
organization can directly cooperate with the environmental protection
departments of local governments in the region to jointly solve the problem
of cross-border environmental protection, thus effectively avoiding the
situation of shirking responsibilities among local governments.

The integration of the local government administrative management
system is inseparable from the construction of regional information plat-
forms. At present, the local government of the metropolitan area of China
and the various departments of the local government are independent of
each other in terms of information platform. There is no effective communication and interaction means between the governments, hindering the
collaboration between local governments and causing asymmetry of
information.[1] By establishing a regional information sharing and exchang-
ing platform, connecting government websites of various local governments and local government departments, and achieving the timely
exchange of information networking and related policy documents, it can
be helpful to the formation of a unified operation platform among the
departments of various local governments, and allow the publication and
sharing of information of various departments on a unified platform, thus
creating conditions for rapid exchanges between local governments and
breaking barriers between governments and departments.

The construction of collaborative governance information platform
includes three aspects. First, establishing an information support system
for cross-regional governance, linking database resources of local governments, and providing information and data supports for local governments
in the metropolitan area, private sectors and non-governmental organizations involved in regional governance, so as to achieve "real-time monitoring, early warning" and other functions for public affairs such as regional
air pollution.[2] The second is to establish a cross-regional information integration mechanism to conduct integration of information on collaborative
governance for regional air pollution, emergency rescue cooperation for
cross-border public crisis events, holistic cooperation on regional water
resources, and important and priority cooperation issues in regional areas
such as transportation and land planning. The third is the establishment of
a cross-regional information service mechanism, providing comprehensive
and convenient information services to enterprises and public in the form
of portals about the policies, regulations and service information concerning government affairs, economic trade and public services of various
local governments in the metropolitan area.[3]

## The construction of cross-jurisdiction collaborative organization

The key to local government collaboration in the metropolitan area is the construction of a cross-jurisdiction holistic collaborative organization, which is the organizational form of holistic governance in the region. In the process of regional governance, whether it is related to river basin or atmosphere issues, it is necessary to establish a special cross-jurisdiction integrated collaborative organization to unify regional ecological and environmental management rights, and specifically responsible for formulating regional strategic plans. Similar institutions have been established in many countries. Such institutions can be either government institutions directly established by the central government or independent legal agents or non-governmental organizations. For example, the establishment of the Tennessee Valley Authority in the United States successfully managed soil erosion, flooding, water pollution and inconvenient transportation in this area through the formulation of a comprehensive management plan for the basin. The Tennessee Valley Authority is a member of the National Assembly and a highly autonomous, financially independent legal entity. In addition to its power to plan within the region, the Authority is also empowered to develop and utilize various natural resources in the basin.[4] In addition, the Murray River Basin Authority of the Murray-Darling River Basin in Australia and the Lerma-Chapala Basin Commission established in the Lerma-Chapala Basin of Mexico have developed corresponding plans based on actual conditions in the region, promoting the coordinated development of the basin.[5]

Among the cross-jurisdiction collaborative organizations established in the metropolitan areas, the Metropolitan Washington Council of Government is comparatively typical. The committee is a regional collaborative organization formed by local governments in the Washington area, consisting of 21 local governments in Washington DC, Maryland and Virginia, plus the representatives of the Maryland and Virginia legislatures, the representatives of US House and the US Senate in the region.[6] All local government members voluntarily join the organization and are ready to withdraw from the alliance. This ensures the voluntariness and fairness of local government members. Its operating funds are mainly financed by local governments, federal and state funding and donations from some foundations and the private sectors. The organization has two main functions, one of which is to allocate federal and state government financial allocations for cross-border public affairs among local government members. US federal law requires that allocations for transportation, housing and environmental protection must be allocated through regional organizations, and local governments that are not members of regional organizations cannot receive financial allocations. This guarantees the legitimacy and authority of the committee. The second is to provide members of local governments with services in the form of public policy research, information dissemination and government wholesale procurement. The committee conducted in-depth researches on issues such as transportation, youth alcoholism and childcare services, providing suggestions for local governments to deal with these social issues. In particular, it is worth mentioning that the committee purchases oil, natural gas and other bulk commodities at a lower price for members, thus saving a lot of administrative expenses for local governments in the region. According to statistics, since the implementation of this plan, the organization has saved at least $1.8 million in annual funding for regional member governments.[7]

Therefore, the construction of the holistic collaborative organization of the metropolitan area must ensure the voluntariness and fairness of the members of various local governments, as well as the legitimacy and authority of the organization itself. On the one hand, cross-regional collaborative organizations need to ensure that local governments can voluntarily join and withdraw. On the other hand, they must obtain the authorization of the central government, and have financial distribution rights and management rights for the special funds for the governance of cross-border public affairs in the metropolitan area. Local governments in the metropolitan area join the cross-regional holistic collaborative organization on a voluntary principle. For each local government, joining and withdrawing from the cross-regional holistic collaborative organization is voluntary, which can enhance the trust of local governments in the collaborative organization. Cross-regional holistic collaborative organizations can be composed of officials from local regional governments, deputies to the National People's Congress, experts and scholars. Representatives from various local governments in the metropolitan area should maintain the same level in quantities so as to ensure the fairness in distributing benefits across regional collaborative organizations. At the same time, the upper level government (including the central government or the provincial government) can give the cross-regional collaborative organization the financial allocation and management rights to the regional public affairs governance, which makes the organization legal. In terms of water resources allocation and environmental pollution control, local governments need to obtain special funds from cross-regional collaborative organizations, which make the collaborative organization have certain authority (see Figure 3.1). And the organization can also set up different special funds for different types of regional collaborative governance. Sources of these funds include funds from higher levels of government,

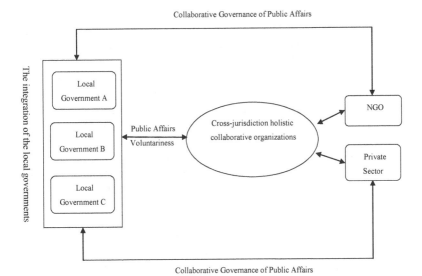

*Figure 3.1* Cross-jurisdiction holistic collaborative organizations.

funds from local governments within the metropolitan area, or contributions from various foundations or the private sector. In this regard, the Washington Metropolitan Government Committee[8] and the establishment of regional special funds of European Union[9] are worth learning. Through the establishment of such organization, it is possible to reduce the costs of information communication, negotiation and distribution, implementation and supervision among various collaborative members in the region. In addition to the construction of this organization, the absorption of NGOs, enterprises and citizens to participate in the governance of regional affairs is also an effective way of governance.

Another important function of the cross-regional holistic collaboration organization is to coordinate the work of various government functions and coordinate the distribution of benefits and compensation among local governments within the region. For example, in the Seine River Basin, France has established a water resources management committee composed of the Ministry of Environment, the Ministry of Communications, the Ministry of Agriculture and the Ministry of Health. It is responsible for formulating the comprehensive management plan for the basin and coordinating the distribution and compensation of benefits in various local governments and departments of the basin.[10] Similarly, European countries have established the Rhine Pollution Control Committee to govern the river Rhine which is flowing across many countries. Its main task is to investigate the pollution and pollutant transport of the Rhine, and promote the implementation of intergovernmental agreements, the implementation of flood control plans and the supervision of sewage emissions from various countries in the basin.[11] In the Ohio River Basin, an agreement was reached between eight states polluted by the Ohio River Basin to form a cross-regional governance institution. The institution is led by a committee of 27 people from the eight states, and its budget is funded through funding from the various district boards. Its responsibility is to coordinate pollution compensation issues in the states.[12]

Therefore, as a cross-regional holistic collaborative organization, it is not only responsible for formulating regional unified planning, but also for the allocation and compensation of regional common interests, which is most prominent in ecological and environmental issues. China's ecological and environmental governance is characterized by the subcontracting governance of various administrative divisions. The vertical management efficiency in the administrative area is relatively high, while the inter-regional horizontal negotiation and management are insufficient, and the administrative separation is obvious. Therefore, it is necessary to establish a unified mechanism for environmental and ecological governance, such as a cross-regional integrated collaborative organization, to plan and coordinate the cooperation of local governments. In addition, there is an urgent need to establish an effective negotiation mechanism in the ecological basin between the upstream local governments, which represents the subject of compensation, and downstream local governments, which represents the object of compensation.[13] In the specific level, the subject with serious loss of interest in the region may apply to the inter-regional holistic collaborative organization for the benefit compensation. The cross-regional holistic collaborative organization may, based on the assessment of the loss, use the special funds jointly funded by local governments within the region to compensate for the ecological damage and environmental pollution. If the subjects are controversial about the loss of interest, the upper level government of the region, such as the central government or the provincial government, can come forward to mediate on this issue and, for the part that is not enough to compensate, organize the re-contribution among the relevant organizations such as the private sector and foundations. Many watershed pollution and agriculture-ecological problems in China are trying to carry out similar solutions. Of course, there is a need to transfer benefits in the area of interest compensation, that is to say, there must be one party in the metropolitan area to transfer interests in terms of interest coordination and compensation.

In the practice of regional collaboration in China, there is a lack of functional departments that are responsible for the implementation of regional policies. Therefore, the construction of cross-regional collaborative organizations is very necessary. Through the construction of this organization, it is possible to actively absorb the NGOs, enterprises and citizens into the governance of regional public affairs. In practice, the Urban Economic Coordination Meeting in the Yangtze River Delta region of China has already established the prototype of a cross-regional collaborative organization.[14] The Yangtze River Delta Urban Economic Coordination Committee plays an important role in the region and actively promotes collaboration of the Yangtze River Delta in financial, medical insurance and modern logistics. Since its establishment in 1997, the coordination committee has so far been continuously expanded to 22 members including Hefei City and Ganzhou City from the first 15 members. What is particularly worth noting is that the Yangtze River Delta Urban Economic Coordination Committee advocates the main role of enterprises in economic cooperation, and at the same time introduces the participation of social intermediary organizations such as associations and chambers of commerce to promote the process of regional integration. On April 18, 2012, the Yangtze River Delta Urban Economic Coordination Committee established the first independent regional collaborative organization in China, namely the Yangtze River Delta Coordination Meeting, thus strengthening the coordination function and executive function of the Mayor Joint Conference during the intersessional period and achieving the institutional construction for regional coordination. This is a good start for China's transition from regional public management to regional governance.[15]

## The establishment of the holistic collaborative governance mechanism

The trust and communication, coordination and compensation, monitoring and evaluation mechanisms between local governments, non-profit organizations and the private sector in the metropolitan area are the basis for achieving integrated collaborative governance. These holistic collaborative governance mechanisms are the link that connects the various subjects in the metropolitan area and also the ways and channels for the collaboration of the various subjects (see Figure 3.2).

In terms of trust and communication mechanisms, through the cautious exploration stage of establishing dialogue and communication channels, the stage of signing contracts for conflicts, and the stage of friendly goodwill that promotes mutual understanding and trust, the gradual construction of trust relationships and communication channels between local governments, non-profit organizations and the private sector in the metropolitan area is the key to collaboration among all these subjects. As far as the interest coordination and compensation mechanism is concerned, vertical fiscal transfer payments, horizontal fiscal transfer payments, private transactions and market trade, public participation mechanisms and eco-labeling policy tools together constitute an interest compensation mechanism for the holistic governance of the metropolitan area. Of course, the relevant policies and regulations formulated by the central government or the upper-level government are the basis for the operation of interest coordination and compensation mechanisms. While cross-jurisdiction holistic collaborative organizations can reduce the costs of information communication, negotiation or distribution, and implementation or super-vision among various collaborative members in the metropolitan area by setting up various special funds and establishing a linkage compensation coordination mechanism, thus dealing with regional interest coordination and compensation issues in a better way. The supervision and evaluation mechanism are the guarantee of the holistic collaborative governance of the metropolitan area. Through the signing of cooperation agreements between local governments, the private sector and non-governmental organizations, the supervision and evaluation on implementation, the supervision and evaluation that vertical level of government conducted for metropolitan collaborative subjects on the collaborative goals and perform-ance, as well as the supervision and evaluation of third-party agents, this mechanism plays a role of guaranteeing the development of regional cooperation.

## The formation of holistic collaborative governance network in metropolitan area

Based on the holistic collaborative governance mechanism, a collaborative network composed of higher-level governments, local governments in the metropolitan area, private sector, non-governmental organizations and inter-regional integrated collaborative organizations is an important way to achieve regional holistic governance (see Figure 3.2). Among them, the local governments in the metropolitan area are the main body of the col-laborative governance network. On the basis of trust and communication mechanism, they reach various agreements on regional public affairs, calculate the benefits and costs in cooperation, reach agreement on interest coordination and compensation, and conduct the supervision and evalu-ation on each other's performance and final results in the process of the contract.

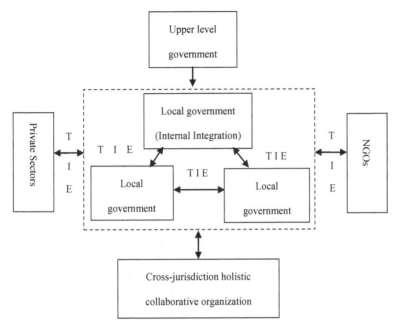

*Figure 3.2* Holistic collaborative governance network.

Notes
T: The mechanism of trust and communication.
I: The mechanism of interest coordination and compensation.
E: The mechanism of monitoring and evaluation.

Second, in order to better achieve regional cooperation, they will also cooperate with the private sector or NGOs in some projects. In cooperation, they also need to establish the trust relationships and distribute the benefits, as well as supervising and evaluating activities. Nonprofit organizations have the characteristics of public welfare nature. At the same time, many non-profit organizations are professional organizations in the fields of environmental protection, transportation, public health, water resources allocation and management. They have strong professional knowledge and abundant practical experience, which can provide the necessary technical and personnel support in solving public affairs for cross-regional holistic cooperation organizations and local governments, thus having obvious advantages in solving public affairs. The private sector is flexible and efficient in addressing cross-border public affairs. By signing contracts with local governments and cross-jurisdiction holistic collaboration organizations, the private sector can address the specific issues of regional public affairs more effectively.

In addition, in this collaborative governance network, the upper level government of the region has the right to manage the network. It participates in the formulation of regional strategic objectives and the guidance of regional policies, coordinates the relationship between regional local governments and also in charge of funding and management of the special funds for regional governance. On this basis, the upper level government is responsible for supervising and evaluating the integrated collaborative governance network. At the same time, in order to cope with the work of the upper-level government, the establishment of a cross-jurisdiction holistic collaborative organization plays a key role in coordinating the intergovernmental relations in the metropolitan area, reducing the communication and distribution costs of each collaborative member, managing and supervising the use of regional funds.

Therefore, in the perspective of holistic governance, the mechanism of trust and communication, interest coordination and compensation, supervision and evaluation among the various subjects in the metropolitan area are the basis for achieving holistic collaborative governance. On the basis of this, the holistic collaborative governance network model of the metropolitan area is undoubtedly an important way to achieve the holistic interests of the metropolitan area and achieve regional inclusive development.

## Conclusion

The holistic collaborative governance model of the metropolitan area includes four parts: the integration of the collaborative governance system and the construction of the information platform; the construction of the inter-regional integrated collaborative organization; the establishment and improvement of the holistic collaborative governance mechanism; the holistic collaborative management network of the metropolitan area.

In response to the administrative barriers existing in the provision of public services by various government departments, local governments in the metropolitan area need to promote the integration of internal institutions and functions in accordance with the principle of functional correspondence, thus forming a unified personnel administration, financial expenditure and information network system within the region. At the same time, it is necessary to establish a regional information sharing and exchange platform to connect websites of various local governments and local government departments, which can create conditions for the rapid exchanges between local governments and break the barriers between governments and departments, so as to establish horizontal integration and linkages between various government departments and its functions.

Cross-jurisdiction holistic collaborative organizations are the organizational form of holistic governance in the metropolitan area. The cross-jurisdiction collaborative organization takes the holistic interests of the region as the starting point, coordinates the integration of different administrative levels and the same level of governments, and cross-departmental collaboration. The organization is built to ensure the voluntariness and fairness of local government members, to ensure the legitimacy and authority of the organization itself, and possess the rights of financial distribution and management for the special funds for cross-border public affairs governance in the metropolitan area.

The mechanism of trust and communication, interest coordination and compensation, supervision and evaluation between local governments, non-profit organizations and the private sector in the metropolitan area are the links that connect the various subjects in the metropolitan area, and are also the ways and channels for the cooperation of various subjects. Based on the holistic collaborative governance mechanism, a collaborative network composed of higher-level governments, local governments in the metropolitan area, private sector, non-governmental organizations and cross-jurisdiction collaborative organizations is an important way to achieve regional holistic governance. Local governments or inter-regional collaborative organizations in the metropolitan area use contract outsourcing, administrative legalization and privatization to establish collaborative relationships with non-profit organizations and the private sector, thus forming a governance network in which local governments and non-profit organizations and private enterprises jointly manage social public affairs.

## Notes

1 Wu Aiming, Cui Jing, Qi Guanghua, "Yunyong dianzizhengwu tuijin xianzhengfu jizhong bangong" ["Promoting the Centralized Work in Municipal and County Governments through E-government"]. *Zhongguo xingzheng guanli* [*Chinese Public Administration*] vol. 5 (2011), 34–37.
2 Zhao Huaying, "huanjing jingjipinkundai zhilizhongde difangzhengfu hengxiang fujihezuo jizhi goujian yanjiu" ["Study on the Construction of Horizontal Inter-Government Cooperation Mechanism of Local Governments in the Governance of the Beijing-Tianjin Poverty Belt"]. *Shanghai shifan daxue shuoshi lunwen* [*Master thesis of Shanghai Normal University*], 2012.
3 Di Lei, "Difangzhengfuxietongzhili de xianzhuangyuqushi" ["The status quo and trend of local government collaborative governance"], in Zhu Guanglei (ed.), *Chinese Government Development Research Report (3rd Series): Local Government Development and Intergovernmental Relations* (Beijing: Zhongguorenmindaxue chubanshe [Beijing: China Renmin University Press], 2013), 140.
4 Hu Yi, Chen Ruilian, "Fadaguojia de liuyushuiwurangonggongzhilijiqi qishi" ["Enlightenment of governance mechanism of water pollution for drainage

66    *The holistic collaborative governance mode*

basin in developed countries"]. *Tianjin xingzhengxueyuanxuebao* [*Journal of Tianjin Administration Institute*] vol. 8, No. 1 (February 2006), 37–40.

5  Chen Ruilian, Rengmin, *Zhongguo liuyuzhili yanjiu baogao* [*Research Report of River Basin Governance in China*] (Shanghai: Gezhi chubanshe [Shanghai: Truth and Wisdom Press], 2011), 242.

6  COG Mission, Metropolitan Washington Council of Government, see www.mwcog.org/community/planning-areas/regional-planning/, accessed on December 30, 2019.

7  H. V. Savitch and R. Vogel, *Regional Politics: American in A Post-city Age* (Thousand Oaks, CA: Sage Publications, 1996), 110, 112.

8  Cui Jing, "Dadushiqu kuajiegonggongshiwu yunxing moshi: fujixiezuo yu zhenghe" ["The Operational Mode of Metropolitan Cross-jurisdiction Public Affairs: The Cooperation and Integration Between Government"]. *Gaige* [*Reform*] vol. 7 (2011), 82–87.

9  Yang Aiping, "Cong chuizhijilidaopingxingjili: difang zhengfuhezuo de liyijilijizhi chuangxin" ["From Vertical Incentive to Horizontal Incentive: As an Innovation of Benefit Encouragement Mechanism in Local Government Cooperation"]. *Xueshuyanjiu* [*Academic Research*] vol. 5 (2011), 47–53.

10 Li Ying, Jiang Guzheng, "Liuyushuiziyuankaifaguihua Zhong zhanluehuanping de zuoyong-yi changjiangkou zonghezhengzhi guihua huanping weili" ["The role of strategic environmental assessment in river basin water resources development planning: A case study of comprehensive environment assessment of the Yangtze River estuary"]. *RenminChangjiang* [*People's Yangtze River*] vol. 8 (2010), 40–42.

11 Yang Zhengbo, "Laiyinhe baohu de guojihezuojizhi" ["International cooperation mechanism for the protection of the Rhine"]. *Shuilishuidiankuaibao* [*Express Water Resources & Hydropower Information*] vol. 1 (2008), 5–7.

12 Hu Yi, Chen Ruilian, "Fadaguojia de liuyushuiwuran gonggongzhili jizhi jiqi qishi" ["Enlightenment of governance mechanism of water pollution for drainage basin in developed countries"]. *Tianjin xingzhengxueyuanxuebao* [*Journal of Tianjin Administration Institute*] vol. 8, No. 1 (February 2006), 37–40.

13 Hu Yi, Li Yuansheng, "Lun liuyu quji shengtaibao hubuchang jizhi de goujian—yi minjiang liuyu weili" ["The Establishment of the Inter-catchment's Ecological Compensation System"]. *Fujian shifandaxuexuebao (zhexueshehuikexue ban)* [*Journal of Fujian Normal University (Philosophy and Social Sciences Edition)*] No. 6 (2006), 53–58.

14 Ye Lin, "Xin quyuzhuyi de xingqiyufazhan: yigezongshu" ["A Review of Literature on New Regionalism"]. *Gonggongxingzhengpinglun* [*Public Administration Review*] vol. 3 (2010), 175–190.

15 Xinhuawang, "Changsanjiao chengshijingji xietiao huicheng guonei shouge duli bangong quyu hezuo zuzhi" ["Yangtze River Delta Urban Economic Coordination Association became the first independent office cooperation organization in China"], see http://news.xinhuanet.com/fortune/2012-04/18/c_111803470.htm, accessed on April 18, 2012.

# 4 Local government collaboration in environmental governance

## Factors affecting collective action

In recent years, regional ecological issues, such as cross-boundary river pollution, air pollution and sandstorms etc., are gradually becoming the focus of the public in China. As a natural ecological whole, the metropolitan area requires collaboration among local governments in terms of cross-boundary environmental issues. However, in practice, there are many difficulties in cross-boundary ecological collaborative governance. Why do the local governments lack cooperation or even fail to cooperate in solving ecological problems with regional common interests? Why do some local governments allow "spillover goods" such as air pollution and water pollution to flow to other areas? These are the important issues to be solved urgently in the collaborative governance of metropolitan areas.

Based on the theory of collaborative governance of local governments, this chapter explores the factors affecting the collective action of local governments in environmental governance from the perspective of the most prominent environmental governance issue in metropolitan collaboration. In addition, it attempts to interpret the dilemma of Chinese-style environmental governance cooperation from the perspective of institutional collective action and to analyze that how do the common interests of ecological collaboration governance of local governments, the preference differences on the overall goal, the attributes of public goods in ecological governance and the asymmetry of local government's strength promote or restrict the collaboration of local governments in environmental governance. It also discusses how the Chinese political tournament of local officials over-inspires the "negative spillover" of ecological governance and under-excites its "positive spillover," which ultimately leads to the dilemma of cross-boundary cooperation within metropolitan area. Based on the analysis of the typical case of the emergence and governance of the poverty belt around Beijing and Tianjin, this chapter reflects on the dilemma of regional ecological collaboration governance in China.

## "Economy based on administrative region," "administrative subcontracting system" and the political tournament of local officials

With regard to the dilemma of cross-boundary environmental governance in the metropolitan area, the existing literature provides three different interpretations. One of the interpretations is that due to the unique administrative and fiscal decentralization system in China, local governments have gained more autonomy and local governments at all levels have formed the "economy based on administrative region" in order to maximize their own interests. The vicious competition and industrial isomorphism among local governments are serious and the division of labor among cities is gradually weakened. The economy in the border area of the administrative regions is relatively exhausted and the cross-regional mobility is seriously hindered.[1] Local government is no longer just an extension of the functions of the central government, but has become an independent market interest subject with more consideration of the "internality" of local economic growth, while less consideration of the external issues such as sustainable development and environment protection.[2] "Economy Based on Administrative Region" leads to competition among local governments, which is becoming increasingly fierce under the background of decentralization and the market economy.[3] Some scholars have put forward the concept of "administration based on administrative region" and believe that the existence of "administration based on administrative region" is the main reason for the formation of administrative division. It is necessary to change this divisional state and achieve the governance of public issues within the region.[4]

Second, "administrative subcontracting system" matching with the administrative and fiscal decentralization, has a long history in China. The relationship among governments is like layer-by-layer subcontracting and the administrative and economic management affairs are subcontracted from the central government to the lowest level of government step by step. As the ultimate contractor, the grass-roots government implements various government matters.[5] As a decentralized governance model with indirect control, administrative subcontracting system makes each local government form its own unique interest structure and often forms "collusion" among them in response to policies and directives from higher authorities.[6] Due to the lack of effective supervision, it is difficult to measure the performance of local governments in environmental governance.

The authoritative relationship and the distribution of control rights between the central government, the intermediate government and the grass-roots government in which the principal party, the management party and the agent party formed by the "administrative subcontracting system" also affect the performance of regional ecological governance.[7] Therefore, whether in the "economy based on administrative region" or "administrative subcontracting system," the dilemma of cross-boundary environmental governance can be explained as the local government's neglect of cross-boundary ecological governance caused by the Chinese-style fiscal and administrative decentralization system.

Another interpretation emphasizes that the competition and cooperation of local governments in public affairs are mainly resulted from the choice of local government leaders under the unique game of political promotion in China. That is to say, the political tournament of local officials at all levels around GDP growth is an important factor in explaining the incentives of local governments.[8] In the political tournament for promotion, local officials, for the sake of their positions and ranks in promotion, are motivated not only to do things that are good for economy in their region, but also to do things that are not beneficial for the region where their competitors are located.[9] This kind of promotion of political tournaments insufficiently motivates the cooperative behaviors with positive spillover effects for local officials. For example, local governments are not interested in the cooperation for cross-boundary road paving and other public goods. While for the behaviors with negative spillover effects, for example the cross-boundary river pollution, such political tournaments may have excessive incentives for the local officials.[10] From this point of view, the political tournament for the promotion of local official in China is an important reason for the dilemma of local government cooperation in the regional environmental governance.

The above three interpretations explain the dilemma of regional environmental governance in varying degrees. Especially the political tournament mode of Chinese officials provides strong theoretical support for us to explore the collaboration among local governments in the environmental governance of metropolitan area. However, as a collective action, the collaborative behavior among local governments in metropolitan area is affected by many factors, which is the result of many games. Therefore, this chapter tries to argue the factors that promote or hinder the collaboration of local governments in environmental governance from the perspective of institutional collective action, so as to explain the dilemma of Chinese-style ecological governance in a new perspective.

The collaboration among local governments in metropolitan area is a kind of regional collective institutional action, that is, several agencies work together to achieve their common policy objectives.[11] Olson argues that collective action occurs when individuals join a group for personal gain and engage in collective behavior.[12] But this often happens in small groups, and collective action by regional local governments as large groups becomes more difficult, because group members are often less aware of the direct benefits of participation and cooperation, and the collective action cost of large groups is higher. In this case, group members are more likely to avoid responsibility such as free riding behavior. The collaborative behavior of regional local governments is also affected by the size of collaborative members and the spatial relationship among them. Therefore, the collective action of local governments in regional environmental governance will be affected and constrained by many factors. Stephanie S. Post also believes that due to incentives such as political promotion, the attitude of local government leaders toward regional collaboration will also promote or hinder regional local government collaboration.[13]

Based on this, this chapter tries to answer three questions. First, what are the preconditions for the collaboration of local governments in environmental governance? Second, which key factors affect the collaboration of local governments in the metropolitan area? Third, how to explain the dilemma of local government collaboration in China's metropolitan area?

## The collective action of local governments in environmental governance

### *The preconditions of intergovernmental collaboration in environmental governance*

Generally speaking, the local governments in the metropolitan area have high homogeneity in geography, river basin, climate and other aspects, that is to say, they are closely dependent on each other, which makes local governments have the motivation to solve common environmental problems.[14] However, there are still several preconditions for local governments in metropolitan area to achieve intergovernmental collaboration in environmental governance:

First, it is necessary for local governments in metropolitan areas to share resources and risks.[15] The ecological problems such as water and air pollution will affect the entire region rather than individual local government. Therefore, only if local governments could realize the necessity of cooperative governance for solving regional environmental problems and the possible serious consequences of non-cooperation, could local governments have the basis for collaboration.

Second, there must be complementary resources and advantages among local governments in metropolitan area. If some local governments in the metropolitan area have resources or geographical advantages that other governments do not have, and these resources are necessary for other governments to solve environmental problems, then collaboration will be possible.[16] For China's Yangtze River Delta, Pearl River Delta and Beijing-Tianjin-Hebei metropolitan areas, it is obvious that the resources and advantages are complimentary in the region. For instance, for other cities in the Yangtze River Delta, it is evident that Shanghai city plays a radiating and driving role in economic development, while Suzhou, Wuxi, Hangzhou and other cities are closely connected with Shanghai and achieve economic complementarity. Another example is the key role of Hebei provincial cities in ecological governance of water supply and sand protection for Beijing and Tianjin city, as well as the economic radiation effect of Beijing and Tianjin city for Hebei Province. This shows complementary characteristics of resources and advantages in Beijing-Tianjin-Hebei metropolitan area.

Finally, the previous experience of collaboration between some local governments within metropolitan area will also have an impact on current and future collaboration.[17] Only in a region where local governments have a good basis for collaboration, can a more effective mechanism of collaboration and consultation be formed for solving environmental problems. If the parties in the metropolitan area have a close relationship and have a good cooperation in history, it is easier to establish a trust relationship. If the history of collaboration is weak, or there is no previous basis for collaboration, the establishment of such cooperative trust will be guaranteed by the guidance of the higher level government and the specific regulations. The basis of collaboration in China's metropolitan areas is different. Some have a long history of collaboration and the trust of all parties in collaboration is relatively easy to establish, such as the Yangtze River Delta and the Pearl River Delta, while others have a short history of collaboration and less experience of collaboration. Therefore, in terms of environmental governance, the trust between local governments in the metropolitan area needs to be further cultivated. When the local governments have no history of collaboration before, they must be willing to take some risks to achieve collaboration.[18] That is to say, collaboration should begin with small steps toward some medium-term goals. Such a successful experience will enhance the trust of all partners in the process of cooperation, thus leading them to develop deeper and broader cooperation.

### *Factors affecting collective action of local governments in environmental governance*

Generally speaking, the geographical density of local governments in metropolitan area will affect their collaboration. A geographic concentration of local governments will increase the likelihood of contact and repeated interaction among local officials in multiple jurisdictions; increase the likelihood that residents will live, work and recreate across multiple jurisdictions, which creates political incentives for cooperation; and increase the likelihood of policy spillovers across local governments in a metropolitan area. These possibilities create incentives for cooperation between local governments.[19] In addition, the group size of local governments is perhaps the important determinant of collective action. The size of the group dictates the ease with which groups can distribute benefits and monitor member behavior. The smaller the group, the lower the management cost and the less lazy members; as the number of organizations included in the group increases, the transaction costs increase.[20] Thus, the greater the number of local governments, the higher the cost of the organization, the less the benefits of distribution and the easier it is to hitchhike. In the case of a certain density and scale of the metropolitan area, the factors affecting the collective action of local governments are as follows:

The first critical feature is that there must be joint gains from collaboration. The larger the aggregate gains, the more likely a cooperative solution.

> There is a simple rationality claim, asserting that cities will not change service arrangement unless each benefits from doing so. The more serious the underlying problem, the larger the aggregate gains from resolving it, and the greater the likelihood of a cooperative arrangement to do so.[21]

This condition has most often been noted in the resolution of environmental problems in metropolitan area. As losses from overconsumption increase, all local governments involved become more likely to seek an agreement to restrict use.[22] Second, it is possible to establish a cooperative relationship only when the aggregate gains exceed the aggregate costs. The greater the margin, the greater the ability of the collective provides selective incentives or attracts a political entrepreneur to organize the group.[23]

In the collaboration of environmental governance, the joint gains among local governments are obvious. However, even if the potential for aggregate gains are large, conflict over the distribution of the gains can prevent any cooperation. The allocation of these joint gains will be affected by the level of asymmetry between parties in their preferences and political strengths. In the process of collaboration, joint gains are necessary but far from sufficient in establishing collaborative relations.[24]

The second characteristic that can affect a collaborative outcome is preference diversity among the participants in environmental collaboration governance. Diversity can exist in that local governments may disagree over the goal of environmental policy or may agree with the overall goal but disagree over the division of the policy outcome. This situation is similar to a zero-sum game, where one city's win means the other must lose. The conflict and competition will define the situation.[25] Cities in metropolitan area always compete with each other to attract the public "good" (like new business) and to avoid the public "bads" (like locally unwanted land uses).

For example, in the governance of the Bohai Sea environment in China's Bohai Rim region, Tianjin city, Hebei province, Shandong province and other different stakeholders often have a dilemma of zero-sum game. Since each local government is paying attention to the economic growth and economic strength of the region, they have competed for limited resources in the Bohai Sea region. In order to develop the economy, the local governments in the upper reaches have let enterprises in the jurisdictions discharge pollutants, and even encourage enterprises to compete for "environmental resources," while the local governments in the lower reaches are suffering from major economic losses caused by water pollution.[26] For another example, local governments in the metropolitan area are reluctant to accept the construction of NIMBY (Not In My Back Yard) facilities such as waste treatment plants, landfills, substations and other neighboring facilities.[27] NIMBY is considered to be public "bads," whose costs are borne by a small number of people but the benefits are enjoyed by most people. Therefore, the NIMBY policy is a regional public policy with the nature of conflict.[28] In this sense, a city will try to avoid building the NIMBY facilities in its own jurisdiction and hope to build them in other cities. The city forced to accept the unwanted land use suffers a loss, while other cities benefit. This kind of behavior of "seeking benefits and avoiding disadvantages" among the local governments in the metropolitan area is reflected in the overall goal of the regional policies.

The third feature is the attribute of public goods of local governments in environmental collaboration governance. The attributes of public goods managed by the metropolitan area are different so the possibility of cooperation between local governments is also different. First, in terms of specific ecological governance policies, such as pastures, fisheries and water resources management, all belong to the governance of public pond resources. Such items have obvious non-exclusive and competitive characteristics. After reaching the "crowding point," each additional person will reduce the utility of the original consumer. For the governance of such goods, local governments in the metropolitan area may agree to sign a cooperation agreement to improve the use of such items by members of the whole region. But the rivalrous nature of the good and the lack of exclusion within the compact make it difficult to determine how much profit this cooperation can bring to each participant, and how much loss this cooperation can make each participant bear. Regional cooperation, in this case, depends on the relationship between the value of the cooperative outcome and each city's ideal outcome. A city government would choose to cooperate if the gain from the cooperative outcome over the status quo is greater than the forgone gain between this outcome and his ideal result.[29] Second, if certain goods or services of environmental cooperative governance of local governments in the metropolitan area have the attributes of obtaining benefits from scale economy and monitoring output easily, then such goods or services are more likely to be collectively produced or publicly provided, such as urban sewage discharge, garbage collection, etc. Such services or goods usually require large-scale production and therefore achieving cost savings from economies of scale. Such products have high input costs that create a barrier to entry for many small local governments. Therefore, small local governments often cannot produce such goods and services themselves.[30] If they want to provide these types of goods and services to their residents, they must either work collectively with each other or they must contract with larger local governments or private vendors.[31] Therefore, cost saving from scale economy is the main economic motivation for local governments to sign contracts. In addition, because the output of such public goods is easier to monitor, the cost and benefit are easier to calculate, and the negotiation cost is relatively low, many local governments are willing to sign cooperation contracts. For instance, regional cooperation projects such as sewage discharge and garbage collection are divisible, tangible, easy to measure and competitive in consumption. Metropolitan area residents are generally uniform in their expectation that clean water will come from their faucets and that solid waste and sewage will be removed from their home, all at a reasonable price. Therefore, a fair market within the region can be established and the costs can be calculated by the benefits of user fees.[32] As a result, local governments could be easier to collaborate on such services.

The fourth characteristic that can affect a collaborative outcome is the asymmetry of local governments' positions and strengths. Generally speaking, the influence of each local government in the metropolitan area is different. It is uncertain under which circumstances cooperation agreements may be signed between local governments with stronger influence, between local governments with weaker influence, and between local governments with stronger influence and weaker influence. Generally, in environmental governance, collaboration between stronger and weaker local governments is possible, because weaker participants have few feasible alternatives and so may be more likely to accept the only deal available.[33] But if the stronger players attempt to extract most of the financial gains, the weaker local governments will feel "exploited" and will not join in the cooperation agreement.[34] In environmental governance, such as air governance and water governance, for symmetric players, their bargaining when signing the cooperation agreement will result in less financial benefits reaped from a cooperative agreement, but participant homogeneity tends to reduce the political transaction costs so that the agreement may still be profitable.[35]

## *The political tournament of local official's promotion: constraints of ecological collaboration of local governments in metropolitan areas*

The factors affecting collaboration, whether are common interests of local governments in the metropolitan area, different attributes of public goods in collaborative governance, or the asymmetry of local government's strength, may be changed or diverted by "filtering" or "refraction" of the political tournament model of local officials' promotion in China. Some factors that contribute to cooperation, which are literally true in intergovernmental relations, will be distorted by the restrictions of such mechanism. It argues that promotion incentives of local government officials can influence inter-regional collaboration in the theory of political tournament of local official's promotion.[36] In China's current GDP-led promotion mechanism, local officials in the management of local affairs will more consider their relative position with the competitors in the promotion, that is, the main start point for thinking about the problems is whether or not affecting promotion rank, rather than the necessity of ecological collaborative governance and the attributes of public goods. Therefore, in the ecological governance cooperation of the metropolitan area, it is easy to achieve cooperation between the cities with strong influence and the cities with weak influence. Because in political tournament, local officials in a region with large economic gaps do not have to worry about changes in their economic position and political gains after cooperation in that the stronger cities and the weaker ones are probably not in the same political competition group. [37] Comparatively, cooperation among strong cities or among weak cities in the metropolitan area will be more difficult in that the benefits of cooperation among members with balanced influences (i.e., the impact of the relative ranking of developments in the two regions after cooperation) are uncertain, so that there is not enough incentive for local officials to cooperate, especially for public goods or services with positive spillover effects, while there is excessive incentive for public goods or services with negative spillover.

The theory of regional collaboration holds that some public goods have the continuity of cross-boundary services, and the greater the continuity, the greater the possibility of local government cooperation. The desire for continuity of services across different local government boundaries is an incentive for another local government to reach a collaborative agreement.[38] Metropolitan governments often strive to ensure seamless provision of public goods and services in the region. For example, the highways should not stop at the boundaries of a city, and watershed protection and forest resource protection should not exist only within a certain city, so cities need the cooperation to ensure consistency in cross-border transport and the basin system. However, the need for ecological collaboration does not necessarily make local governments have a strong impetus for cooperation in that cooperation is also dependent on the position expectation of local officials in the promotion game. There may be cooperation between stronger and weaker city governments, while local officials in strong or weak city governments are reluctant to cooperate with each other even if the ecological government issues they faced are continuous and cross-boundary, because they are worried that cooperation will bring more benefits to other cities and affect their own promotion.

In addition, the theory of regional collaboration believes that the policies of many local governments will generate spillovers benefits and costs to local governments in the vicinity, and these "extra spillover effect between local governments" provide powerful incentives for signing intergovernmental agreements. But in the theory of political promotion game, "spillover effect" does not work as an incentive for cooperation. In order to improve their own political performance while reducing the position of competitors, local governments are not very keen on collaborations with positive spillover effect, such as forest resources protection and the construction of trans-boundary sewage facilities which are beneficial to the whole metropolitan area. While for the cooperation with negative spillover effect, such as cross-border river pollution, the incentives are excessive. That is to say, if the water pollution within the jurisdiction can affect the production of enterprises in adjacent competitive areas, in order to gain an advantage in the promotion competition, local officials will indulge and protect the pollution behaviors of enterprises in the region from the motive of "sabotage," leading to the phenomenon of "beggar thy neighbor," which is often seen in the cross-boundary river pollution governance.[39] However, the excessive incentives for such negative spillovers in the promotion game, or the unscrupulous "vicious competition," will also make the economic development at the border areas of various provinces or cities become a "cold shoulder." Because all local governments are worried that due to their geographical proximity, the efforts of environmental

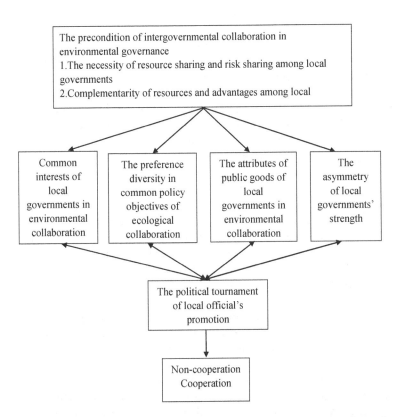

*Figure 4.1* Factors affecting collective action of local governments in environmental governance.

protection such as water resources and forest resources protection in their border areas will spill over to the adjacent competitive areas, which leads to the unreasonable use of water resources, forest resources and other public resources in the border areas of provinces and regions, resulting in the problem of water pollution and excessive development.[40]

## The governance of the poverty belt around Beijing and Tianjin

In recent years, after the Pearl River Delta and the Yangtze River Delta, repaid development of the Beijing-Tianjin-Hebei Metropolitan Area has attracted more and more attention. However, along with the economic development, the Pearl Delta and the Yangtze River Delta have driven the development of the surrounding rural areas, while a large poverty belt around Beijing and Tianjin has been formed. In 2005, Asian Development Bank published a report entitled "Research on Economic Development Strategy of Hebei Province," which clearly proposed the concept of "poverty belt around Beijing and Tianjin" for the first time. According to the report, in Beijing-Tianjin-Hebei Metropolitan Area, there are 32 poverty-stricken countries in the C-type area surrounding the two munici- palities of Beijing and Tianjin, distributing in Yanshan Mountain and Bashang areas of Zhangjiakou and Chengde, Taihang Mountain area (in the scope of Baoding city) west of the Beijing-Guangzhou Railway, and Heilonggang flow area of Cangzhou, etc. The economic development level of these poverty-stricken counties is far lower than the average level of poverty-stricken counties in China, which is one of the areas with the greatest disparity in economic development in the eastern coastal areas of China.[41] It is rare that such poverty exits in an area just over 100 kilo- meters away from metropolis like Beijing and Tianjin. Therefore, the poverty belt around Beijing and Tianjin has been focused by the academia and the public, and it is also a typical case of the dilemma in environ- mental collaborative governance.

Scholars have many explanations about the causes of the poverty belt around Beijing and Tianjin. On the one hand, one of the basic reasons for the formation of the poverty belt is its fragile ecological environment, such as poor natural conditions, water shortage and serious soil degradation.[42] Indeed, the poverty belt around Beijing and Tianjin, located in the semi- arid and semi-humid transitional climate zone in China, is a region where the desertification of Bashang grassland and the fossilization of Yanshan and Taihang mountains are serious, and where there is a barren alkali land in Heilonggang, a poor area for hundreds years. Due to the restrictions on natural geographical condition and insufficient self-development ability, many poor areas have fallen into a vicious circle of "poverty-plundering exploitation-ecological deterioration-the root of regional poverty."[43] On the other hand, the polarizing effect of Beijing and Tianjin on Hebei prov- ince is greater than the diffusion effect, which is also an important reason for the formation of poverty belt.[44] Since the reform and opening up, due to the "siphon" effect of Beijing and Tianjin, the capital, talents, raw materials and other resources in regions surrounding Beijing and Tianjin have flowed to the two municipalities while the poverty-stricken areas are not only unable to benefit from the "location advantages" around metro- politan area, but are further deprived of various resources, aggravating poverty.[45] What is more, the decentralized management model and non- market resources allocation make the poverty and environment in the region continue to deteriorate.[46] As is located in the eastern part of China, especially adjacent to Beijing, Zhangjiakou and Chengde, two cities in the poverty belt around Beijing and Tianjin have failed to enter the "preferential policies circle" in every national adjustment of the regional development strategy. No matter "the western development," "the revitalization of old industrial bases in northeast," "the rise of central China" or other strategies, failed to take into account this "blind zone."[47] As a result, this region has received less policy support.

However, all these factors reflect the awkward predicament of local governments in the metropolitan area of Beijing, Tianjin and Hebei in the process of regional environment collaboration, such as urban water reply, sandstorm source control and atmospheric environment management. Why are the areas adjacent to the two metropolitan areas suffering from the double pressures of environmental degradation and poverty, instead of benefiting from the economic radiation? To answer these questions, we need to explore the influencing factors of regional environmental collaboration.

For the Beijing-Tianjin-Hebei Metropolitan Area, there are preconditions of environmental collaborative governance within the region. Beijing, Tianjin and Hebei province not only have the necessity of ecological environment sharing and risk sharing such as water resources, atmospheric resources and sand control, but the complementarity of resources and advantages. It is particularly important that the dry rivers and lakes, soil erosion and pollution, grassland degradation, forest destruction and other phenomena in the Beijing-Tianjin-Hebei Metropolitan Area have seriously affected the urban water supply and the atmospheric environment in that region. In recent years, the negative effects of poverty-stricken ecological problems in poverty belts around Beijing and Tianjin on the Beijing-Tianjin-Hebei region have become increasingly apparent, such as recurring water supply crises and severe sandstorms in Beijing, Tianjin and Tangshan.[48] The existence of such weakness also restricts the coordinated development and regional integration of the Beijing-Tianjin-Hebei Metropolitan Area. At the same time, the existence of a large number of poverty-stricken people around Beijing and Tianjin will result in the influx of low-quantity labor force into big cities, forming urban poverty population centers, which will bring certain difficulties to the city management.[49] Therefore, although there are sufficient preconditions for the coordination of ecological governance in the Beijing-Tianjin-Hebei Metropolitan Area, the necessity and urgency of collaborative governance do not necessarily form a valuable collaboration. In environmental collaborative governance of the Beijing-Tianjin-Hebei Metropolitan Area, the factors promoting or hindering regional cooperation are intertwined and interact with each other, affecting the final collaborative results.

First of all, the fundamental conflict of interest in ecological governance of local governments in the region is an important reason for the emergence of the poverty belt around Beijing and Tianjin, that is to say, the existence of zero-sum game makes local governments "seek benefits and avoid disadvantages." Although the ecological problems around Beijing and Tianjin region are so serious that the development of all parties is threatened, and local governments also realize that collaborative governance has common interests for this region. In practice, however, it is difficult to ensure a Pareto optimum result in which each participant must at least be able to benefit from cooperation. In this kind of zero sum game, the benefit of one city inevitably means the loss of another, Hebei Province around Beijing and Tianjin has made a lot of benefit concessions and sacrifices for Beijing and Tianjin in the aspects of water resources, sand control, etc. For a long time, Hebei Province, where the poverty-stricken zone around Beijing and Tianjin is located, has been the ecological barrier of Beijing and Tianjin area, shouldering the tasks of blocking sandstorm, water supply and water quality purification for Beijing and Tianjin. In the Beijing area, 81 percent of the water and 94 percent of the water in Tianjin area are supplied by Hebei Province.[50] In order to ensure the water supply and sand control, the water source of Hebei province has shut down numerous enterprises with considerable benefits, serious water consumption and low sewage standards, reduced irrigated land, and implemented the projects of forest conservation, returning the grain plots to forestry and grass in controlling area of wind and sand, which means the industrial, agricultural and animal husbandry industries in the poverty-stricken area around Beijing and Tianjin area have suffered huge losses. In recent years, especially around 2008, in order to create a good ecological environment for the Beijing Olympic Games and ensure the clean air in the capital, Beijing has relocated many heavily polluting enterprises, such as Shougang (Capital Steel and Iron Works) and Beijing Coking Plant, to the surrounding Hebei Province, while the people who moved to the area are suffering from the negative consequences of the pollution of "adjacent facilities."

Second, why local governments in Hebei province, under the zero-game, do not choose the strategy of "seeking the advantages and avoiding the disadvantages"? This refers to another factor affecting ecological collaboration of local governments, namely the asymmetry of local governments' strength. Beijing, as the capital of China, and Tianjin, as one of the important economic centers in northern China, are the key areas of national development both in history and after the founding of P. R. China. This means local governments around Beijing and Tianjin in Hebei province, have no alternative for cooperation, and are unlikely to gain too much from the bargaining due to the unequal influence. For example, Guanting Reservoir, jointly built by Hebei and Beijing, is one of the main water sources in Beijing, and Hebei province also enjoys a certain share of water. The construction of this project occupied 113 square kilometers of land in Hebei Province, relocated 41,600 people, and suffered a direct economic loss of 660 million yuan. However, when Beijing began to run out of water in 1980s, Hebei gave up its water consumption of 900 million cubic meters per year. At the same time, since the Luan-Jin water transfer project was deployed in 1983, the Panjiakou reservoir in Hebei supplies 1 billion cubic meters of water to Beijing per year. So far, the area around Beijing and Tianjin in Hebei Province, which belongs to the arid and water deficient area in the north, has to pay for water from the Yellow River while providing its own water resources to Beijing and Tianjin free of charge.[51] For another example, in order to ensure the quality of water supplied to Beijing and Tianjin, Zhangjiakou city shut down the Xuanhua paper mill, which has contributed more than 50 million yuan of profit and taxes every year, and more than 6 million yuan every year to cover the basic living expenses of more than 3500 unemployed workers in the factory.[52] However, in order to protect and support the development of Beijing and Tianjin, most of these losses of industry, agriculture and animal husbandry are borne by the local governments and people in Hebei Province, the transfer payments from the central government are insufficient, and the compensation from Beijing and Tianjin are temporary and unable to make up for the huge losses in the area around Beijing and Tianjin. It is particularly important that Beijing-Tianjin-Hebei Metropolitan Area, different from the Pearl River Delta and the Yangtze River Delta, has prominent administrative system obstacles within the region, and coordination between vertical and horizontal local governments is difficult. At present, the cross-boundary ecological compensation mechanism has not been established, which makes the poverty problems in Beijing and Tianjin region more and more obvious.

In addition, the ecological management of water resources and pastures in the area around Beijing and Tianjin belongs to the management of "public pond" resources, which have the characteristics of "crowding point," that is, after reaching a certain level, each additional use will reduce the utility of the original customers. The competitiveness and lack of exclusiveness of the public goods reduce the willingness of cooperation between regional governments. At the same time, the output of this kind of public pond resource goods is not easy to monitor, the cost and benefit are not easy to calculate, and the negotiation cost is high, so many local governments are not willing to sign cooperation contracts. In this case, the deterioration of ecological environment and poverty problems in the poverty belt around Beijing and Tianjin are intertwined, that is, the poverty-related ecological problems and the ecology-related poverty problems. After decades of water supply and sand control, the ecology of the poverty-stricken area around Beijing and Tianjin has become very fragile and sensitive, and the deterioration of the ecological environment, such as river drying up, wetland and spring disappearing, soil erosion and pollution, is also very serious. In turn, the circular relationship between economic poverty and ecological deterioration restricts the long-term and sustainable development of Beijing and Tianjin, and threatens the ecological security of Beijing and Tianjin and the realization of the goal of building an international metropolis.

Finally, the formation of poverty belt around Beijing and Tianjin is a result of local officials' promoting incentives in the metropolitan area.[53] According to the "political incentive and constraints of economic cooperation" proposed by the game model of political promotion, the closer the economic strength is, the more difficult it is to cooperate. In the Beijing-Tianjin-Hebei metropolitan area, there are always difficulties in the competition and coordination of positioning between Beijing and Tianjin. For example, in regional cooperation, Tianjin is keen to promote the "vertical" regional mechanism. The joint meeting of Mayors for regional cooperation around the Bohai Sea advocated by Tianjin has been held for 16 times, while Beijing has only participated in the joint meeting of mayors as an "observer" and is unwilling to live under Tianjin, and has translated the "vertical" to the "horizontal" mode, that is, the one-to-one cooperation mode signing agreements with some cities in Hebei Province. Therefore, the competition between the two cities around who is the leader in Bohai Sea Ring area makes the incentives for local officials to promote ecological governance collaboration relatively weak, because what local officials consider is whether collaboration will affect their relative rankings, and then worry about whether the cross-domain and positive spillovers of ecological governance will benefit other free riders if they collaborate. This kind of promotion game of local officials in two cities made them not keen on ecological governance cooperation that has common interests in the region, and led to Beijing-Tianjin area adjacent to them becoming a common "neglected" corner. The ecological resources around Beijing-Tianjin region are over exploited due to the guarantee and supply of Beijing and Tianjin, unable to reasonably protected, but also become an ecological negative spillover inflow area in views of undertaking many pollution enterprises in Beijing and Tianjin.

# Conclusion

There is an interdependent relationship among local governments, which motivates them to solve common ecological issues. However, whether the necessity of cooperative resources sharing and risk sharing in the metropolitan area, or the complementarity between resources and advantages, it does not always lead to an effective cooperation. Local government cooperation in metropolitan area is also influenced by the common interests in collaborative governance, the diverse preferences in overall objectives, the attributes of public goods and the asymmetry of local governments' strength.

From the perspective of collaboration theory, the greater common interests and the more serious potential problems in the region, the greater possibility of cooperation among local governments exists. Of course, common interests require the existence and realization of Pareto Optimum in which none of the participants got worse and at least one participant got better. However, even though local governments in metropolitan area agree that common benefits they obtained are large, the contradictions in distributing benefits will also hinder their cooperation as the distribution of common benefits is influenced by the diverse preferences in the objectives of local government, the attributes of public goods in collaborative governance and the asymmetry of cooperative members' influence. First, it is the diverse preferences in overall objectives of local governments in ecological collaboration governance, or the existence of zero-sum games that makes local governments compete with each other and fight for "environmental resources." While in the areas that are unfavorable to their region, they refuse to each other, allowing cross-boundary water pollution and air pollution and others flow to other regions. As a result, competition will be the mainstream of intergovernmental relations, and regional collaboration is difficult to be established in a short time. Second, the attributes of public ponds resource in ecological collaborative governance may affect local government's cooperation. Despite the governance of such item can bring common interests to the whole region, local governments will weigh costs against benefits because of its exclusivity and competitiveness. Furthermore, in view of the high costs of negotiation and the difficulty in controlling output, local governments are less willing to sign cooperation contracts. Third, the asymmetry of local government's strength also affects cooperation. Generally speaking, the stronger and weaker local governments are the easier it is to reach cooperation, because participants with weaker influence have no choice but to accept the only agreement proposed in the cooperation. In addition, on account of political tournament model in local official's promotion, the collective action in local government's ecological governance is restricted. Under the influence of political promotion game, the cooperation between local governments with strong influence and the local governments with weak influence in the metropolitan area will be more difficult, because local officials with similar influence worry that positive spillovers of environmental governance will flow to the neighboring areas after collaboration, resulting in the change of their own political gains or economic rankings. Correspondingly, the promotion game has over stimulated "negative spillover" of ecological governance, so that local officials let water pollution and air pollution flow to adjacent regions. It is the joint effect coming from "positive spillovers effects" and "negative spillovers effects" that lead to the collaborative dilemma in cross-provincial areas such as poverty belt around Beijing and Tianjin.

How to solve the dilemma of regional ecological collaborative governance in China? Many scholars and local governments are making useful explorations. Whether it is to strengthen the regulation of ecological governance cooperation from the legal level, or to build the collaborative mechanism of cross-domain ecological governance, the collective action of ecological governance should be combined with the following three mechanisms to fundamentally solve the dilemma of Chinese-style local government in regional ecological governance cooperation.[54]

### The establishment of government-led ecological benefit compensation mechanism and the finance transfer payment system

The reason why the cost of cross-boundary cooperation among local governments in metropolitan area is higher is due to the channel of interest coordination for intergovernmental interest compensation and transfer payment not being smooth. The first approach to resolve this problem is to build the government-led ecological benefit compensation and financial transfer payment system. In the regional environmental governance, the construction of environmental facilities and the remediation of water and air pollution can be jointly funded by the local governments either in their region or the upstream and downstream local governments of rivers in the region; or central and local governments can transfer the financial payment to the source area for the eco-environmental project and social and economic development of the source area and the upstream,[55] or the central and regional governments can jointly fund the establishment of special funds to compensate the costs paid by some local governments to protect the environment, including the loss of right to use water resources, the loss of restriction on the development rights and interests of traditional industrial, the local government's loss of improving the regional standard of regional function, and the cost of ecological engineering protection.[56]

## *The establishment of market-oriented water right and pollution right trading mechanism*

The second way to ensure a smooth channel of interest coordination among local governments in metropolitan area is to establish the market-oriented water and pollution right trading mechanism. The premise of this mechanism is to clearly define the water right and emission right in law so as to create a trading market for water right and pollution right.[57] Emission trading is that the government sets the goal of total pollution control and establishes an emission permit system, which makes emission permit become a scarce resource that can be traded in the market. At present, there have been some preliminary explorations, including water rights transactions between two county-level cities, Dongyang and Yiwu in Zhejiang province, and water pollutant emissions trading by the cities of Zhangjiagang, Taicang and Kunshan in the Taihu Lake Basin of Jiangsu province.

## *The enhancement of the ecological indicators in the officials' management performance appraisal system*

In Chinese local officials' promotion incentives, the indicators associated with economic growth and maintaining stability are "hard indicators" with a nature of "one-vote veto." By contrast, incorporating environmental protection indexes such as ecological governance into local governments' performance appraisal system, has just begun piloting in Zhejiang, Sichuan province and Inner Mongolia Autonomous Region of China. Moreover, these environmental indicators are "soft indicators" with no strict binding and have no substantial relationship with local official's promotion. As a result, local governments often sacrifice environmental indexes to achieve other priorities, even manipulate statistics to cope with the assessment of superiors and public's aspiration, under the pressure of political motivation model, thereby evading environmental governance responsibilities.[58] In this case, incorporating ecological environmental indicators into the local official's performance appraisal system and becoming a "hard indicator" with a nature of "one-vote veto," or designing a set of ecological evaluation index system with the core of "Green GDP," is the key to effectively promote the interest coordination between the central and local government as well as among local governments in metropolitan area.[59]

The above analysis of the factors affecting collaborative governance in metropolitan area further demonstrates the necessity of constructing the collaborative governance mechanism of local governments in metropolitan area. However, the collaboration of local government in metropolitan area, not only includes the aspects of ecology and environment, but also covers a large number of public affairs such as transportation, culture, police and tourism, which requires the establishment of a broader collaborative mechanism.

## Notes

1 See Shu Qing, Zhou Keyu, *Cong fengbi zouxiang kaifang: zhongguo xingzhengqu jingji toushi* [*From Closed to Open: Perspective of The "Administrative Regional Economy" in China*] (Shanghai: Huadong shifan daxue chubanshe [Shanghai: East China Normal University Press], 2004) and Liu Junde, "Zhongguo zhuanxingqi tuxian de xingzhengqu jingji xianxiang fenxi" ["Analysis on the Prominent 'Administrative Regional Economy' Phenomenon in China's Transitional Period"]. *Lilun qianyan* [*Theory Frontier*] Vol. 10 (2004).

2 Yu Minjiang, "Lun shengtai zhili zhong de zhongyang he difang zhengfu jian liyi xietiao" ["Interests Coordination Between Central and Local Governments in Environmental Governance"]. *Shehui kexue* [*Social Sciences*] Vol. 9 (2011).

3 Feng Xingyuan, "Lun xiaqu zhengfu jian de zhidu jingzheng" ["Study on Inter-jurisdictional Institutional Competition"]. *Guojia xingzheng yueyuan xuebao* [*Journal of Chinese Academy of Governance*] Vol. 6 (2001).

4 Yang Aiping, Chen Ruilian, "Cong xingzhengqu xingzheng dao quyu gonggong guanli: zhengfu zhili xingtai shanbian de yizhong bijiao fenxi" ["From Administering Administrative Districts to Regional Public Administration: A Comparative Analysis of the Evolution of Governmental Forms to Governance"]. *Jiangxi shehui kexue* [*Jiangxi Social Sciences*] Vol. 11 (2004).

5 Zhou Lian, *Zhuanxing zhong de difang zhengfu: guanyuan jili yu zhili* [*Local Government in Transition: Officials' Incentive and Governance*] (Shanghai: Shanghai renmin chubanshe [Shanghai People's Publishing House], 2008).

6 Zhou Xueguang. "Jiceng zhengfu jian de gongmou xianxiang: yige zhengfu xingwei de zhidu luoji" ["Collusion among Local Governments: The institutional logic of a government behavior"]. *Shehuixue yanjiu* [*Sociological Studies*] Vol. 3 (2008).

7 Zhou Xueguang, Lian hong, "Zhongguo zhengfu de zhili moshi: yige kongzhiquan lilun" ["Modes of Governance in the Chinese Bureaucracy: A 'control right' Theory"]. *Shehuixue yanjiu* [*Sociological Studies*] Vol. 5 (2012).

8 Zhou Lian, "Zhongguo difang guanyuan de jinsheng jinbiaosai moshi yanjiu" ["Governing China's Local Officials: An Analysis of Promotion Tournament Model"]. *Jingjiyanjiu* [*Economic Research Journal*] Vol. 7 (2007).

9 Zhou Lian, "Jinsheng boyi zhong zhengfu guanyuan de jili yu hezuo: jianlun woguo difang baohu zhuyi he chongfu jianshe de wenti" ["The Incentive and Cooperation of Government Officials in the Political Tournaments: An Interpretation of the Prolonged Local Protection and Duplicative Investments in China"]. *Jingji yanjiu* [*Economic Research Journal*] Vol. 6 (2004).

10 Zhou Lian, *Zhuanxing zhong de difang zhengfu: guanyuan jili yu zhili* [*Local Government in Transition: Officials' Incentive and Governance*] (Shanghai: Shanghai renmin chubanshe [Shanghai People's Publishing House], 2008).

11 Stephanie S. Post, "Metropolitan Area Governance and Institutional Collective Action," in Richard C. Feiock (ed.), *Metropolitan Governance: Conflict, Competition, and Cooperation* (Washington, D.C.: Georgetown University Press, 2004), 70.

12 Mancur Olson, *The Logic of Collective Action* (Cambridge, MA: Harvard University Press, 1965).

13 Stephanie S. Post, "Metropolitan Area Governance and Institutional Collective Action," in Richard C. Feiock (ed.), *Metropolitan Governance: Conflict, Competition, and Cooperation* (Washington, D.C.: Georgetown University Press, 2004), 79.

14 Jeanne M. Logsdon, "Interests and Interdependence in the Formation of Problem-Solving Collaborations," *Journal of Applied Behavioral Science*, Vol. 27, No. 1 (1991).

15 Catherine Alter and Jerald Hage, *Organizations Working Together* (Newbury Park, CA: Sage Publications, 1993).

16 Barbara Gray and Donna Wood, "Collaborative Alliances: Moving from Practice to Theory," *Journal of Applied Behavioral Science*, Vol. 27, No. 1 (1991).

17 Beryl A. Radin, Robert Agranoff, Ann O' M Bowman, et al., *New Governance for Rural America: Creating Intergovernmental Partnerships* (Lawrence: University Press of Kansas, 1996).

18 Sivan Vgen and Chris Huxham, "Nurturing Collaborative Relations: Building Trust in Interorganizational Collaboration," *Journal of Applied Behavioral Science*, Vol. 39, No. 1 (2003).

19 Stephanie S. Post, "Metropolitan Area Governance and Institutional Collective Action," in Richard C. Feiock (ed.), *Metropolitan Governance: Conflict, Competition, and Cooperation* (Washington, D.C.: Georgetown University Press, 2004), 73.

20 Oliver Williamson, *Market and Hierarchies* (New York: Free Press, 1975).

21 Annette Steinacker, "Game-Theoretic Models of Metropolitan Cooperation," in Richard C. Feiock (ed.), *Metropolitan Governance: Conflict, Competition, and Cooperation* (Washington, D.C.: Georgetown University Press, 2004), 47–48.

22 See Mark Lubell, Mark Schneider, John Scholz and Mihriye Mete, "Watershed Partnerships and the Emergence of Collective Action Institutions," *American Journal of Political Science*, Vol. 46, No. 1 (2002); Elinor Ostrom, *Governing the Commons* (New York: Cambridge University Press, 1990); Elinor Ostrom, Roy Gardner and James Walker, *Rules, Games, and Common-Pool Resources* (Ann Arbor: University of Michigan Press, 1994).

23 See Mancur Olson, *The Logic of Collective Action* (Cambridge, MA: Harvard University Press, 1971) and Russell Hardin, *Collective Action* (Baltimore, MD: Johns Hopkins University Press, 1982).

24 See Gary Lipecap, *Contracting for Property Rights* (New York: Cambridge University Press, 1989) and Willian Riker and Itai Sened, "A Political Theory of the Origin of Property Rights: Airport Slots," *American Journal of Political Science*, Vol. 35, No. 4 (1991).

25 Annette Steinacker, "Game-Theoretic Models of Metropolitan Cooperation," in Richard C. Feiock (ed.), *Metropolitan Governance: Conflict, Competition, and Cooperation* (Washington, D.C.: Georgetown University Press, 2004), 48–49.

26 Cui Lu, Wang Shuming, "Study on the Low Efficiency Trans-boundary Watershed Environmental Policy in China-An Example of Benefit Mechanism Analysis of Basin Management in Bohai Rim Region" in *Di san jie quanguo keji zhexue ji jiaocha xueke yanjiusheng luntan wenji* [*The Third National Philosophy of Science and Technology and Interdisciplinary Graduate Forum*], (2010).

27 NIMBY, also known as the locally unwanted land use (LULU), usually refers to somewhere in the area to build some of physical health, environmental quality and bring many negative impacts of facilities like the value of the asset, such as waste treatment plants, landfills, coal-fired power plants, substations, incineration plant, etc.

28 R. W. Waste, *The Ecology of City Policymaking* (New York: Oxford University Press, 1989).

29 Annette Steinacker, "Game-Theoretic Models of Metropolitan Cooperation," in Richard C. Feiock (ed.), *Metropolitan Governance: Conflict, Competition, and Cooperation* (Washington, D.C.: Georgetown University Press, 2004), 49.

30 See Vincent Ostrom, Charles Tiebout and Robert Warren, "The Organization of Governance in Metropolitan Areas: a Theoretical Inquiry," *American Political Science Review*, Vol. 55 (1961); Robert Stein, *Urban Alternatives: Public and Private Markets in the Provision of Local Services* (Pittsburgh, PA: University of Pittsburgh Press, 1990); James Ferris and Elizabeth Graddy, "Contracting Out: For What? With Whom?" *Public Administration Review*, Vol. 46, No. 4 (1986).

31 Robert Stein, *Urban Alternatives: Public and Private Markets in the Provision of Local Services* (Pittsburgh, PA: University of Pittsburgh Press, 1990).

32 Stephanie S. Post, "Metropolitan Area Governance and Institutional Collective Action," in Richard C. Feiock (ed.), *Metropolitan Governance: Conflict, Competition, and Cooperation* (Washington, D.C.: Georgetown University Press, 2004), 78.

33 Annette Steinacker, "Game-Theoretic Models of Metropolitan Cooperation," in Richard C. Feiock (ed.), *Metropolitan Governance: Conflict, Competition, and Cooperation*, Washington, D.C.: Georgetown University Press, 2004, 50–51.

34 Richard Thaler, "Anomalies: The Ultimatum Game," *Journal of Economic Perspectives* Vol. 2, No. 4 (1988).

35 Raymond Deneckere and Carl Davidson, "Incentives to Form Coalitions with Bertrand Competition," *RAND Journal of Economics*, Vol. 16, No. 4 (1985).

36 Zhou Lian, "Jinsheng boyi zhong zhengfu guanyuan de jili yu hezuo-jianlun woguo difang baohu zhuyi he chongfu jianshe de wenti" ["The Incentive and Cooperation of Government Officials in the Political Tournaments: An Interpretation of the Prolonged Local Protection and Duplicative Investments in China"]. *Jingji yanjiu* [*Economic Research Journal*] Vol. 6 (2004).

37 Zhou Lian, *Zhuanxing zhong de difang zhengfu: guanyuan jili yu zhili* [*Local Government in Transition: Officials' Incentive and Governance*] (Shanghai: Shanghai renmin chubanshe [Shanghai People's Publishing House], 2008).

38 Stephanie S. Post, "Metropolitan Area Governance and Institutional Collective Action," in Richard C. Feiock (ed.), *Metropolitan Governance: Conflict, Competition, and Cooperation* (Washington, D.C.: Georgetown University Press, 2004), 70.

39 Zhou Lian, *Zhuanxing zhong de difang zhengfu: guanyuan jili yu zhili* [*Local Government in Transition: Officials' Incentive and Governance*] (Shanghai: Shanghai renmin chubanshe [Shanghai People's Publishing House], 2008), 257.

40 Zhou Lian, *Zhuanxing zhong de difang zhengfu: guanyuan jili yu zhili* [*Local Government in Transition: Officials' Incentive and Governance*] (Shanghai: Shanghai renmin chubanshe [Shanghai People's Publishing House], 2008), 256.
41 Yang Lianyun, Li Hongmin, "Huan jingjin pinkundai de xianzhuang yu fazhan zhanlue yanjiu" ["Research on the Present Situation and Development Strategy of the Poverty Belt around Beijing and Tianjin"] in Jing Tihua (ed.), *2005–2006 zhongguo quyu jingji fazhan baogao* [*2005–2006 Annual Report on China's Regional Economy*] (Beijing: Shehui kexue wenxian chubanshe [Beijing: Social Sciences Academic Press], 2006).
42 Zhao Yu, "Dui huan jingjin pinkundai de fuchi buchang jizhi yanjiu" ["Research on the Support and Compensation Mechanism of the Poverty Belt around Beijing and Tianjin"]. *Jingji wenti yanjiu* [*Inquiry into Economic Issues*] Vol. 3 (2008).
43 Research Group, Poverty Belt around Beijing and Tianjin Issue, "Dui huan jingjin pinkundai fazhan xianzhuang yu duice de genzong yanjiu" ["Tracking Research on the Development Status and Countermeasures of the Poverty Belt around Beijing and Tianjin"] in Qi Benchao, Jing Tihua (ed.), *2009–2010 zhongguo quyu jingji fazhan baogao* [*2009–2010 Annual Report on China's Regional Economy*] (Beijing: Shehui kexue wenxian chubanshe [Beijing: Social Sciences Academic Press], 2010).
44 Chen Lie, Sun Haijun, Zhang Surong, "Jiyu ditan jingji de huanjingjin pinkundai fazhan moshi yanjiu" ["Research on Development Model of the Poverty Belt around Beijing and Tianjin Based on Low Carbon Economy"]. *Fazhan yanjiu* [*Development Research*] Vol. 6 (2012).
45 Research Group, Poverty Belt around Beijing and Tianjin Issue, "Dui huan jingjin pinkundai fazhan xianzhuang yu duice de genzong yanjiu" ["Tracking Research on the Development Status and Countermeasures of the Poverty Belt around Beijing and Tianjin"] in Qi Benchao, Jing Tihua (ed.), *2009–2010 zhongguo quyu jingji fazhan baogao* [*2009–2010 Annual Report on China's Regional Economy*] (Beijing, Shehui kexue wenxian chubanshe [Beijing: Social Sciences Academic Press], 2010), 176.
46 Lu Da, Pan Haitao, "Huan jingjin pinkundai fachu jingshi zhi yan" ["The poverty Belt around Beijing and Tianjin Gives Warning Words"]. *Zhangguo gaige bao* [*China Reform News*] (September 19, 2005).
47 Research Group, Poverty Belt around Beijing and Tianjin Issue, "Dui huan jingjin pinkundai fazhan xianzhuang yu duice de genzong yanjiu" ["Tracking Research on the Development Status and Countermeasures of the Poverty Belt around Beijing and Tianjin"] in Qi Benchao, Jing Tihua (ed.), *2009–2010 zhongguo quyu jingji fazhan baogao* [*2009–2010 Annual Report on China's Regional Economy*] (Beijing, Shehui kexue wenxian chubanshe [Beijing: Social Sciences Academic Press], 2010), 177.
48 Research Group, Regional Cooperation in the Poverty Belt around Beijing and Tianjin, "Xiaochu huanjingjin pinkundan, cujin jingjinyi quyu xietiao fazhan" ["Removal of the Poverty Belt around Beijing and Tianjin, Promotion of the Coordinated Development of the Beijing-Tianjin-Hebei Region"] in Jing Tihua (ed.), *2004–2005 zhongguo quyu jingji fazhan baogao* [*2004–2005 Annual Report on China's Regional Economy*] (Beijing, Shehui kexue wenxian chubanshe [Beijing: Social Sciences Academic Press], 2010), 177.
49 Yang Lianyun, Li Hongmin, "Huan jingjin pinkundai de xianzhuang yu fazhan zhanlue yanjiu" ["Research on the Present Situation and Development Strategy

of the Poverty Belt around Beijing and Tianjin"] in Jing Tihua (ed.), *2005–2006 zhongguo quyu jingji fazhan baogao* [*2005–2006 Annual Report on China's Regional Economy*] (Beijing: Shehui kexue wenxian chubanshe [Beijing: Social Sciences Academic Press], 2006), pp. 94–95.

50  Liu Guihuan, Zhang Huiyuan, Wang Jinnan, "Huan jingjin pinkundai de sheng-tai buchang jizhi tansuo" ["Study on the Ecological Compensation Mechanism in the Poverty Belt around Beijing and Tianjin"] in *Zhongguo huanjing kexue xuehui xueshu nianhui youxiu lunwenji* [*Proceedings of the Academic Annual Conference of Chinese Environmental Sciences Association*], 2006.

51  Wei Hongxia, "Huan jingjin pinkundai yu jingjin shengtai anquan" [Poverty Belt around Beijing and Tianjin and Ecological Security in Beijing and Tianjin"]. *Hebei linye* [*Hebei Forestry*] Vol. 5 (2006).

52  Zhao Yu, "Dui huanjin pinkundai de fuchi buchang jizhi yanjiu" ["Research on the Support and Compensation Mechanism of the Poverty Belt around Beijing and Tianjin"]. *Jingji wenti yanjiu* [*Inquiry into Economic Issues*] Vol. 3 (2008).

53  Zhou Lian, *Zhuanxing zhong de difang zhengfu: guanyuan jili yu zhili* [*Local Government in Transition: Officials' Incentive and Governance*] (Shanghai: Shanghai renmin chubanshe [Shanghai People's Publishing House], 2008), 252.

54  Cui Jing, "Shengtai zhili zhong de difang zhengfu xiezuo: zi jingjinyi dushi-quan guancha" ["The Collaboration of Local Government on Ecological Governance: from the Prospective of the Metropolitan Area of Beijing-Tianjin-Hebei"], *Gaige* [*Reform*] Vol. 9 (2013).

55  Wang Junfeng, "Zhongguo liuyu shengtai buchang jizhi shishi kuangjia yu buchang moshi tanjiu-jiyu buchang zijin laiyuan de shijiao" ["Research on Implementation Framework of Ecological Compensation Mechanism and Compensation Mode: from the Prospect of Compensation Funds Source"]. *Zhongguo renkou ziyuan yu huanjing* [*China Population, Resources and Environment*] Vol. 2 (2013).

56  Liu Guihuan, Zhang Huiyuan, Wang Jinnan, "Huan jingjin pinkundai de sheng-tai buchang jizhi tansuo" ["Study on Ecological Compensation Mechanism in the Poverty Belt"] in *Zhongguo huanjing kexue xuehui xueshu nianhui youxiu kunwenji* [*Proceedings in Chinese Society for Environmental Sciences*], 2006.

57  Zhou Lian, *Zhuanxing zhong de difang zhengfu: guanyuan jili yu zhili* [*Local Government in Transition: Officials' Incentive and Governance*] (Shanghai: Shanghai renmin chubanshe [Shanghai People's Publishing House], 2008), 257.

58  Ran Ran, "Yalixing tizhi xia de zhengzhi jili yu difang zhengfu huanjing zhili" ["Political Incentives and Local Environmental Governance Under a 'Pressu-rized System'"]. *Jingjishehuitizhi bijiao* [*Comparative Economic & Social Systems*] Vol. 3 (2013).

59  Yu Minjiang, "Lun shengtai zhili zhong de zhongyang yu difang zhengfu jian liyi xietiao" ["Interests Coordination Between Central and Local Governments on Ecological Governance"]. *Shehui kexue* [*Social Sciences*] Vol. 9 (2011).

# 5   The collaborative network among local governments in the Beijing-Tianjin-Hebei metropolitan area in P. R. China

Based on the theory of regional collaborative governance, this chapter measured the degree centrality, betweenness centrality, and closeness centrality of the collaborative network of 13 local governments in the Beijing-Tianjin-Hebei metropolitan area through social network analysis (SNA). Through the cohesive subgroup analysis and the visualized collaborative network described by the UCINET software, the internal structure of the Beijing-Tianjin-Hebei metropolitan area and the interactive mode among members were revealed, and the evolution of this collaborative network was then analyzed. Research results demonstrated that this local government collaborative network does not have high overall network density but shows a developing trend of high density. The impact of economic and social development radiating out from Beijing and Tianjin, the two core cities, is gradually appearing in the Beijing-Tianjin-Hebei metropolitan area. However, development is still restricted by the local governments of Hebei Province. Chengde, Baoding, Langfang and Zhangjiakou, four prefecture-level cities of Hebei Province, which surrounds Beijing and Tianjin, and take advantage of their location and cooperate with Beijing and Tianjin. They represent an emerging cohesive subgroup of the Beijing-Tianjin-Hebei metropolitan area. Nevertheless, the multi-centered network structure of the Beijing-Tianjin-Hebei metropolitan area is not yet fully formed, resulting in insignificant synergistic effect within the network. Thus, trust, multi-collaborative governance, and benefit distribution and compensation mechanisms should be established as soon as possible in order to improve overall performance and realize regional coordinated development.

Metropolitan governance and local government collaboration have been the focus of considerable interest and investigation by local government and urban scholars since the early 1990s. However, as discussed in a review by LeRoux, Brandenburger and Pandey,[1] while compelling research on local governance and intergovernmental relations has focused on theoretical claims, case studies and anecdotal evidence, it has failed to examine the features and structure of collaboration networks among local governments in depth and discuss which factors could contribute to their collaboration.

Scholars have examined a number of critical issues surrounding metropolitan governance, including why local government collaboration networks are important for regional governance,[2] why institutional collective action matters for interlocal service delivery "through a web of voluntary agreements and associations,"[3] what mitigating mechanisms have evolved for dealing with problems related to collective action,[4] how social networks might shape the opportunities and constraints of the local governments,[5] and which properties characterize collaborative policy networks.[6] Despite considerable attention given to understanding collaborative networks in metropolitan areas by scholars of collaborative public management,[7] the topic is still new and remarkably undeveloped. Even in the area of local government collaboration, there is a significant lack of research on how whole networks evolve.

A second issue that is often neglected in the literature is the conception of the network. It seems that most scholars see it as a collection of public, private and nonprofit agencies which work together to provide public goods and establish shared norms. For instance, some scholars study the formal and informal networks in merged non-profit organizations.[8] However, the interlocal network is believed to be the key to reducing social inequalities and improving local government economic efficiency in metropolitan areas.[9] The local governments themselves should form a voluntary and fluid collaborative network to make regional policy decisions when a metropolitan area is "fragmented,"[10] which would enhance the social and economic relationships among them. Thus, the interlocal network is the focus of this chapter.

Building on these basic ideas, our work was guided by three research questions. First, what is the structure of the local government collaborative network in the Beijing-Tianjin-Hebei metropolitan area? Second, do different structures remain stable over time despite network growth and environmental shifts? Third, how can the effectiveness of this network be improved.

To answer these questions, we conducted a longitudinal study of a local government collaborative network of cross-jurisdiction public affairs. Data were collected in two periods from a single network in the Beijing-Tianjin-Hebei metropolitan area: when the network was first formed in 2004–2007, and again in 2008–2011, after it had matured. Analysis focuses on changes in the patterns of interaction within and across 13 cities.

## Background and hypotheses

Recently, more and more public problems beyond local government juris-diction and functions of government departments occur in metropolitan areas. To solve these problems, government departments gradually extend their efforts beyond boundaries and across levels, leading to increasing reports of cross-cutting cooperation.

New regionalism that advocates cross-sector alliances focuses on con-structing collaborative networks among different levels of government, non-governmental organizations and private sectors through negotiation in order to manage regional public affairs.[11] It supports replacing the single, rigid governmental management mode with flexible horizontal network governance and encourages non-profit organizations, commercial associ-ations and citizens in the region to participate in holistic governance.[12] Feiock and Scholzinvestigate collaborative governance of local govern-ments within the framework of institutional collective action (ICA), paying close attention to higher-order, collective-action problems among authori-ties, such as public goods, natural monopolies and economies of scale as well as the management of public pool resources.[13] LeRoux, Branden-burger and Pandey find that social networks play an important role in the cooperation of local governments in a region.[14] Local government officials are better able to develop ties between local governments by participating in collaborative organizations (e.g., metropolitan committees) and by having the same educational backgrounds (e.g., an MPA degree). Additionally, due to the unequal strength of different local governments within a metropolitan area, efforts to establish cooperation between them are not always successful. Generally speaking, stronger and weaker local governments may cooperate with each other in ecological management. This is because the weaker local government has few feasible alternatives, making it more likely to accept the proposal made by the stronger player.[15] But if the stronger local government attempts to seize most of the benefits, the weaker one will feel it is being "exploited" and will thus be reluctant to accept the cooperation agreement.[16]

In China, water resource allocation, air pollution and cross-regional river pollution have become problems that governments at all levels in the Beijing-Tianjin-Hebei, Yangtze River Delta and Pearl River Delta must face. Nevertheless, it is difficult for local governments to maintain long-term, effective collaborative relationships because of the continuous "fragmentation," or administrative segmentation,[17] the lack of a cross-regional administrative coordinating agency,[18] and imperfect trust, profit distribution and assessment mechanisms.[19] For example, without coordination of cross-regional collaborative organizations like the River

Environmental Protection and Governance Committee, environmental pollution and ecological safety problem in the Yangtze River Delta are increasingly serious. For instance, the river basin area of the Taihu only accounts for 0.38 percent of China's total river basin area, but it contributes 10 percent of the national pollutant discharge capacity. Such serious water pollution causes the widespread "quality-induced water shortage" in the Taihu Basin.[20] Moreover, the management of PM2.5, particles that can go directly into the alveoli of the lungs, highlights the importance of regional collaboration in the Beijing-Tianjin-Hebei metropolitan area with regard to environmental governance. Because of these problems, how to effectively promote collaborative governance of local governments in the metropolitan areas has become a key issue in China's current regional development. Based on previous studies and metropolitan governance practices in China, we proposed two research hypotheses:

Hypothesis 1: In metropolitan areas, cities with higher administrative levels (e.g., centrally administered municipalities) are less influenced by other cities in the collaborative network. Therefore, these cities are assumed to have higher closeness centrality than other cities.

Hypothesis 2: Cities adjacent to "megacity behemoths" are more easily able to serve as "brokers" of the collaborative network of the metropolitan areas. They are able to facilitate the interaction of regional networks to a certain extent, thus leading to higher betweenness centrality than other cities.

## Data and methods

### The research setting

The subject of the research is the Beijing-Tianjin-Hebei metropolitan area, covering two centrally administered municipalities (Beijing and Tianjin) and 11 prefecture-level cities of Hebei Province (Tangshan, Chengde, Zhangjiakou, Baoding, Langfang, Qinhuangdao, Cangzhou, Shijiazhuang, Hengshui, Handan and Xingtai). It is a new regional growth pole in China today. In the decades since China's reform and opening-up policies were first implemented, Beijing, Tianjin and the cities of Hebei Province transitioned from industrial isomorphism and cut-throat competition to preliminary economic and technical cooperation and, these days, to exploration of regional collaborative governance. In 2004, the National Development and Reform Commission (NDRC) called Beijing, Tianjin, Qinhuangdao, Tangshan and five other cities together and arrived at the "consensus of

Langfang," which laid the foundation for collaboration within the Beijing-Tianjin-Hebei metropolitan area.[21] In the same year, the NDRC officially launched the Beijing-Tianjin-Hebei metropolitan planning initiative, which was incorporated into the "11th Five-Year Plan" of Beijing, Tianjin and Hebei Province. Therefore, 2004 is the starting point of our research studying various collaborations among the local governments of Beijing, Tianjin and Hebei Province.

As the national economy and social development entered the "12th Five-Year Plan," the Beijing-Tianjin-Hebei metropolitan area encountered new opportunities. In the "12th Five-Year Plan," Hebei Province not only chose 14 counties that are adjacent to Beijing for the construction of "One Metropolitan, Four Districts, and Six Bases," but also expanded the connections with Beijing in terms of transportation, communications, finance and social security.[22] As a central city, Beijing also proposed in the "12th Five-Year Plan" that it should play an increasingly important role in regional development. In 2006, the "11th Five-Year Plan" had admitted the Tianjin Binhai New Area into the national strategy. In that same year, the State Council had decided to gradually make Tianjin part of the economic center of Northern China and required Tianjin to be coordinated with Beijing. In 2014, collaborative development of Beijing, Tianjin and Hebei Province was elevated to the national strategic level, laying the foundation for further local government cooperation.

## Data collection

In this study, data from 2004 to 2011 on various collaborations of 13 local governments in the Beijing-Tianjin-Hebei metropolitan area were collected as study samples. Based on the theory of collaborative governance of metropolitan areas, social network analysis (SNA) was used to investigate the structure, characteristics and performance of the collaborative network of these local governments. For the sake of convenience, the names of cities in the following tables and figures are expressed using their initials in Chinese Pinyin: Beijing (BJ), Tianjin (TJ), Shijiazhuang (SJZ), Tangshan (TS), Handan (HD), Xingtai (XT), Hengshui (HS), Cangzhou (CZ), Zhangjiakou (ZJK), Chengde (CD), Qinhuangdao (QHD), Langfang (LF) and Baoding (BD).

Our main research data were collected from official cooperation contracts signed by the local governments of the Beijing-Tianjin-Hebei metropolitan area and from data records of city interaction. These records came from bilateral visits and inspections by senior administrative heads of local governments, collaborative meetings, forums and organizations cooperating in public affairs, such as transportation, public health, law enforcement and environmental management. To analyze the changes in the role of each city in this collaborative network, these data were divided into two periods for comparison: 2004–2007 and 2008–2011 (Table 5.1). As every collaborative behavior of cities involves interaction of two or more related parties, this collaborative network was an undirected network.

In the SNA, network density, degree centrality, betweenness centrality and closeness centrality were measured using UCINET Version 6.126 software to analyze the structure and features of the network. Through the cohesive subgroups analysis and the visualized collaborative network described by Net Draw in the UCINET software, the internal structure of the Beijing-Tianjin-Hebei metropolitan area and interaction modes of members were revealed, and the evolution of the collaborative network was analyzed.

## Results

The network density of the Beijing-Tianjin-Hebei metropolitan area during 2004–2007 and 2008–2011 was calculated by UCINET software, which reported 0.1632 and 0.2414 respectively, indicating low overall network density. In other words, the local governments of the area are not closely collaborating with each other. As a new metropolitan area, the scope and depth of the collaboration of the local governments of Beijing, Tianjin and Hebei Province in public affairs such as culture, the environment and transportation should be improved. However, these results also show that the density of the collaborative network is gradually increasing, signifying increasing cross-jurisdiction communication in the Beijing-Tianjin-Hebei metropolitan area, which in turn has an increasing impact on the behaviors of local governments.

The degree centrality of the collaborative network of the Beijing-Tianjin-Hebei metropolitan area reflects the capability of one city to develop ties with other cities. The overall degree centrality of this collaborative network during 2004–2007 and 2008–2011 was calculated by UCINET as 8.73 percent and 12.73 percent, respectively. This demonstrates that the local governments of the Beijing-Tianjin-Hebei metropolitan area have actively established collaborative relationships with other cities. Table 5.2 shows the degree centrality of each city of the Beijing-Tianjin-Hebei metropolitan area in the collaborative network. Beijing has the highest degree centrality (26.0) during 2004–2007, which implies its central position in the collaborative network. This is the result of a series of policies promoting Beijing-Tianjin-Hebei regional development after the implementation of China's reform and opening-up policies as well as

*Table 5.1* Collaboration and interaction data of 13 cities of the Beijing-Tianjin-Hebei metropolitan area from 2004 to 2011

| City | BJ | TJ | SJZ | TS | HD | XT | HS | CZ | ZJK | CD | QHD | LF | BD |
|---|---|---|---|---|---|---|---|---|---|---|---|---|---|
| BJ | 0 | 109 | 80 | 88 | 77 | 77 | 76 | 83 | 84 | 88 | 81 | 93 | 86 |
| TJ | 109 | 0 | 80 | 88 | 77 | 78 | 77 | 88 | 78 | 84 | 87 | 92 | 83 |
| SHZ | 80 | 80 | 0 | 77 | 76 | 76 | 73 | 77 | 74 | 78 | 77 | 78 | 79 |
| TS | 88 | 88 | 77 | 0 | 77 | 76 | 73 | 79 | 76 | 81 | 82 | 79 | 79 |
| HD | 77 | 77 | 76 | 77 | 0 | 76 | 73 | 76 | 73 | 76 | 76 | 76 | 76 |
| XT | 77 | 78 | 76 | 76 | 76 | 0 | 73 | 76 | 73 | 77 | 77 | 76 | 76 |
| HS | 76 | 77 | 73 | 73 | 73 | 73 | 0 | 73 | 73 | 73 | 73 | 73 | 73 |
| CZ | 83 | 88 | 77 | 79 | 76 | 76 | 73 | 0 | 75 | 79 | 79 | 80 | 78 |
| ZJK | 84 | 78 | 74 | 76 | 73 | 73 | 73 | 75 | 0 | 79 | 75 | 76 | 78 |
| CD | 88 | 84 | 78 | 81 | 76 | 77 | 73 | 79 | 79 | 0 | 79 | 81 | 79 |
| QHD | 81 | 87 | 77 | 82 | 76 | 77 | 73 | 79 | 75 | 79 | 0 | 79 | 78 |
| LF | 93 | 92 | 78 | 79 | 76 | 76 | 73 | 80 | 76 | 81 | 79 | 0 | 80 |
| BD | 86 | 83 | 79 | 79 | 76 | 76 | 73 | 78 | 78 | 79 | 78 | 80 | 0 |

Beijing's clustering effect as the primary city of the region. From the preliminary proposal of establishing an economic collaboration region surrounding Beijing and Tianjin as well as an economic and technological collaboration region in northern China to the later "Capital Economic Circle," and then to integrating the "Beijing-Tianjin-Hebei Metropolitan Plan" launched by NDRC into Beijing's "11th Five-Year Plan", Beijing's central position in the Beijing-Tianjin-Hebei regional network has increasingly been emphasized. Furthermore, many large enterprises, both foreign-owned and domestic, such as Korean Pohang Iron & Steel Company (POSCO) and Honric Group, have established headquarters in Beijing, further highlighting Beijing's position as a city for global headquarters.

Tianjin shows the highest degree centrality in the collaborative network (38.0) during 2008–2011, far higher than that of Beijing during 2004–2007. This means that the position of Tianjin in the regional network has become prominent, or perhaps that the dual-core structure of the Beijing-Tianjin collaboration had been formulated. In 2006, the State Council approved Tianjin Binhai New Area as the National Comprehensive Reform Pilot Area, which conferred the rights of reforming the market economic, financial and social management systems to Tianjin.

Moreover, degree centrality in Table 5.2 shows that Langfang, Tangshan, Chengde, Baoding, Cangzhou and Qinhuangdao of Hebei Province have strong competence in the collaborative network of the Beijing-Tianjin-Hebei metropolitan area. This is mainly because they are able to take full advantage of their locations, being adjacent to Beijing and Tianjin and able to accept some industries and commercial markets transferred from the central cities. Due to urban development, several pollution-producing factories, including the Capital Steel and Iron Corporation and the Beijing Internal Combustion Engine Plant, have moved to Hebei Province, primarily to the prefecture-level cities surrounding Beijing (e.g., Langfang and Baoding).

The overall betweenness centrality of cities in the Beijing-Tianjin-Hebei metropolitan area is not very high, 2.39 percent (2004–2007) and 1.58 percent (2008–2011), respectively. As shown in Table 5.2, Tianjin achieves the highest betweenness centrality from 2004 to 2007, while Tianjin and Beijing show the highest betweenness centrality from 2008 to 2011. This reveals that Tianjin plays the role of "broker" in the network and many collaborations in the region are implemented through it. Tianjin has in fact been promoting the establishment of regional collaboration mechanism. The 16-session "Mayor Joint Conference of Economic Association in Bohai Coastal Region" launched by the Tianjin government is the only institutionalized regional collaboration in the Beijing-Tianjin-Hebei region. In addition, *Tianjin's Promotion of Bohai Coastal Regional*

*Table 5.2* Centrality statistics of the collaborative network of 13 cities in the Beijing–Tianjin–Hebei metropolitan area

| Rank | Degree centrality | | | | Between centrality | | | | Closeness centrality | | | |
|---|---|---|---|---|---|---|---|---|---|---|---|---|
| | Rank | 2004–2007 | Rank | 2008–2011 | Rank | 2004–2007 | Rank | 2008–2011 | Rank | 2004–2007 | Rank | 2008–2011 |
| 1 | BJ | 26.00 | TJ | 38.00 | BJ | 10.00 | TJ | 6.75 | QHD | 5.254 | BJ | 5.556 |
| 2 | TJ | 24.00 | BJ | 35.00 | TJ | 4.50 | QHD | 6.75 | TJ | 5.254 | TJ | 5.556 |
| 3 | LF | 15.00 | TS | 19.00 | CD | 4.50 | CD | 1.75 | CD | 5.254 | CD | 5.545 |
| 4 | ZJK | 12.00 | CD | 17.00 | BD | 0.00 | BJ | 1.75 | BJ | 5.244 | BD | 5.545 |
| 5 | TS | 12.00 | BD | 17.00 | TS | 0.00 | HD | 0.00 | LF | 5.244 | TS | 5.534 |
| 6 | CZ | 12.00 | LF | 16.00 | HD | 0.00 | XT | 0.00 | BD | 5.244 | HD | 5.534 |
| 7 | CD | 10.00 | CZ | 16.00 | HS | 0.00 | HS | 0.00 | SJZ | 5.244 | SJZ | 5.534 |
| 8 | QHD | 10.00 | QHD | 16.00 | CZ | 0.00 | CZ | 0.00 | CZ | 5.244 | CZ | 5.534 |
| 9 | SJZ | 9.00 | SJZ | 10.00 | ZJK | 0.00 | ZJK | 0.00 | ZJK | 5.244 | LF | 5.534 |
| 10 | BD | 9.00 | HD | 10.00 | SJZ | 0.00 | SJZ | 0.00 | TS | 5.244 | XT | 5.534 |
| 11 | XT | 2.00 | XT | 10.00 | QHD | 0.00 | TS | 0.00 | XT | 5.169 | QHD | 5.534 |
| 12 | HS | 1.00 | ZJK | 4.00 | LF | 0.00 | LF | 0.00 | HS | 5.160 | ZJK | 5.472 |
| 13 | HD | 0.00 | HS | 2.00 | XT | 0.00 | BD | 0.00 | HD | 0.00 | HS | 5.451 |

*Cooperation* in 2006, *Comments on Establishing a Coordinated Communication Mechanism for Promoting Beijing-Tianjin-Hebei Metropolitan Development* in 2008 and *Shenyang Proposal of Bohai Coastal Regional Collaboration* in 2010 are all efforts of the Tianjin government. Of all the cities in Hebei Province, Chengde has the highest betweenness centrality in 2004–2007 and 2008–2011, indicating that Chengde is another important hub city in the Beijing-Tianjin-Hebei metropolitan network. Many collaborative affairs are accomplished through Chengde.

Closeness centrality of cities in the Beijing-Tianjin-Hebei metropolitan area is generally low, but distributed evenly. This reveals that all members of this collaborative network are "controlled" by other cities to a considerable degree, but the overall network connections have been formed. From 2004 to 2007, Qinhuangdao, Tianjin and Chengde have higher closeness centrality, but it is Beijing and Tianjin that achieve higher closeness centrality from 2008 to 2011. This demonstrates that as a new metropolitan area, the core city position of Beijing and Tianjin in this metropolitan area has been consolidated since 2008. They are superior to other cities in resources, reputation and power.

In addition, Chengde and Baoding have higher closeness centrality than other cities in Hebei Province, indicating that they have closer collaborative ties with central cities in the regional network and less dependence on or are less influenced by other cities in the network. In contrast, Hengshui, Handan and Xingtai are far away from the central cities in the network and their developments are restricted by other cities.

## Discussion and conclusions

The collaborative network of the Beijing-Tianjin-Hebei metropolitan area has 13 urban nodes. Matrix data in Table 5.1 were divided into two groups (2004–2007 and 2008–2011) and then entered into Net Draw in UCINET, generating two visual networks of local government collaboration (see Figures 5.1 and 5.2). The arrow lines between cities in Figures 5.1 and 5.2 represent the collaborative relationship between them. The evolution of the collaborative network of local governments can be seen clearly in the visual networks.

First, the connections of the collaborative network of the Beijing-Tianjin-Hebei metropolitan area were strengthened from 2004–2007 to 2008–2011. In Figures 5.1 and 5.2, it can be seen clearly that from 2004 to 2011, a regional collaborative network was established preliminarily in the Beijing-Tianjin-Hebei metropolitan area. This is in line with China's adjustment and planning of regional space structure after 2005. With the launch of the "11th Five-Year Plan," a total of six core economic circles

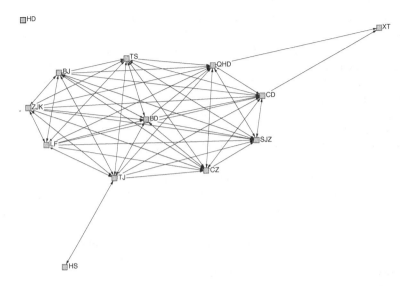

*Figure 5.1* Visual network of local government collaborations in the Beijing-Tianjin-Hebei metropolitan area from 2004 to 2007.

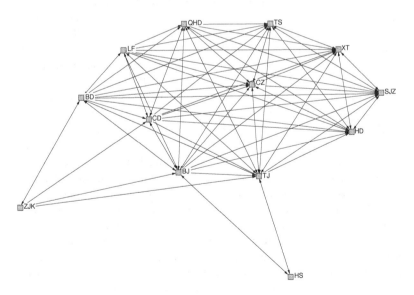

*Figure 5.2* Visual network of local government collaborations in the Beijing-Tianjin-Hebei metropolitan area from 2008 to 2011.

were successively formed in China. Among them, the development of the capital economic circle and the Bohai coastal economic circle accelerated the integration of the Beijing-Tianjin-Hebei metropolitan area and gave birth to the *Beijing-Tianjin-Hebei Metropolitan Plan.* Driven by these core economic circles, China's strategy shifted from a non-equilibrium regional development strategy favorable for coastal regions to a coordinated regional development strategy.[23] The local governments of the Beijing-Tianjin-Hebei metropolitan area, relieved from their early competitive relations, began to establish preliminary economic and technological cooperation and then built cross-jurisdictional collaborations in public affairs.[24]

Second, the horizontal relationship among members of regional collaborative network changes continuously. The multicenter metropolitan network is not yet fully formed, thus showing insignificant synergistic effect. In Figure 5.1, the collaborative network of BJ, TJ, BD and eight other cities shows a high degree of aggregation, while XT and HS are not closely related with the regional network. It is important to note that HD is isolated from the regional collaborative network and has established few collaborative relationships with other cities in the region. However, with accelerating urban and regional integration, the horizontal relationship among cities of the Beijing-Tianjin-Hebei metropolitan area has changed accordingly. In Figure 5.2, HD has already integrated into the regional collaborative network and is closely related with other cities. HS maintains essentially the same position in the network, still not so closely related with the regional network. To sum up, compared to the mature metropolitan areas like the Pearl River Delta and Yangtze River Delta, the collaboration of local governments in the Beijing-Tianjin-Hebei metropolitan area is too weak to improve the overall performance of network governance.

Cliques of subgroups in the Beijing-Tianjin-Hebei metropolitan collaborative network were analyzed by UCINET, providing the subgroup structures in the network (Figures 5.3 and 5.4). Through the analysis of cliques in the collaborative network, we can not only attain a good understanding on how every city in the Beijing-Tianjin-Hebei metropolitan area is embedded into the network but also analyze the closeness between cities and changes to subgroups with time and spatial alternation.

It can be seen in Figure 5.3 that from 2004 to 2007, the collaborative network of the Beijing-Tianjin-Hebei metropolitan area was preliminarily formed, developing two general subgroups. One was in Hebei Province including Qinhuangdao, Chengde and Xingtai.[25] The other was comprised of Beijing, Tianjin, Shijiazhuang, Tangshan, Cangzhou, Zhangjiakou, Langfang and Baoding. During this period, Beijing and Tianjin did not influence the region significantly. Hengshui and Handan, at the southern

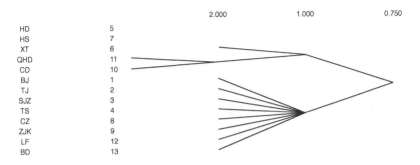

*Figure 5.3* Subgroup structure of the Beijing-Tianjin-Hebei metropolitan collaborative network from 2004 to 2007.

border of Hebei Province, did not embed into either of the above subgroups because they are far from Beijing and Tianjin and thus rarely col-
laborated with other cities.

Figure 5.4 illustrates how the subgroup structure of the collaborative
network changed in 2008–2011. Two large subgroups were formed. One
was the subgroup surrounding Beijing and Tianjin and included Chengde,
Baoding, Beijing, Tianjin and Zhangjiakou. In the other subgroup, Langfang, Qinhuangdao and Tangshan drove Shijiazhuang, Handan, Xingtai
and Cangzhou. Furthermore, Hengshui began to be involved in the collaborative network and established more and more ties with other cities in the
metropolitan area. Chengde and Baoding, in the first subgroup, connected
with Beijing and Tianjin frequently, taking full advantage of their geographic positions. They serve as an important bridge for public affairs collaboration between Beijing/Tianjin and other cities in Hebei Province.
Particularly, with the proposal of Hebei's "Green Economic Circle
surrounding the Capital," four prefecture-level cities (Chengde, Baoding,

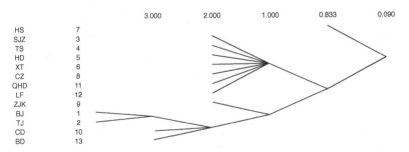

*Figure 5.4* Subgroup structure of the Beijing-Tianjin-Hebei metropolitan collaborative network from 2008 to 2011.

Zhangjiakou and Langfang) surrounding Beijing have become important places into which Beijing and Tianjin's urban function expands. In the second subgroup, Qinhuangdao, Tangshan and Cangzhou, as coastal cities in Hebei Province, connect Beijing with the Liaoning coastal economic zone surrounding the Bohai Sea, the Tianjin Binhai New Area and the Yellow River Delta High-Efficiency Ecological Economic Zone. After the *Development Plan of Coastal Regions in Hebei Province* was approved by the State Council in 2011, Qinhuangdao, Tangshan and Cangzhou have become important places for industrial transfers from Beijing and Tianjin. The annual "Northeast Asian and Bohai-rim International Cooperation Forum" held in Langfang has become more and more influential since 2004. The linking role of Langfang in the collaborative network has gradually become prominent. As a result, a regional governance network centered at Beijing and Tianjin is developing in the Beijing-Tianjin-Hebei metropolitan area, while the functions of other cities in the network remain indistinct and the multicenter subgroups unformed. The cities must further enhance their communication, interaction and collaboration efforts.

In short, in this chapter, we have analyzed the collaborative network composed of 13 cities in the Beijing-Tianjin-Hebei metropolitan area through SNA. Based on three proposed problems and two research hypotheses, we come to the following conclusions: (1) The local government collaborative network of the Beijing-Tianjin-Hebei metropolitan area does not have high overall density but shows a developing trend of high density. (2) The effect of economic and social development radiating from Beijing and Tianjin continues to grow gradually. Their degree centrality is always higher than that of 11 cities in Hebei Province. However, their closeness centrality was not high from 2004 to 2007 and did not reach its highest point until 2008–2011. Therefore, Beijing and Tianjin are highly dependent on the cities in Hebei Province, and their developments are restricted by the developments of local governments in Hebei Province. This partially proves Hypothesis 1. (3) Tianjin and Chengde are key connectors and "brokers" in the collaborative network of the Beijing-Tianjin-Hebei metropolitan area. They facilitate the formation of the collaborative mechanism of the regional network to a large extent. In contrast, Langfang is not recognized as an important "broker." This partially proves the Hypothesis 2.

This research has important implications for the Beijing-Tianjin-Hebei metropolitan area. First, to promote further integration of the metropolitan area, it is necessary to build a trust mechanism among the local governments. Building trust among the various interested parties in the metropolitan network is the premise of local government collaboration in the Beijing-Tianjin-Hebei region. In the metropolitan area, previous competition between Beijing and Tianjin makes it imperative to build a trust mechanism within the current collaborative network. This process should include several progressive phases. The first is a cautious level of trust. Cities in the metropolitan network could open communication channels for collaboration. Through these preliminary communications, city governments could get a general understanding of basic political, economic and cultural conditions as well as some collaboration commitments. The second stage involves building mutual understanding and trust. After tentative communications, local governments in the metropolitan area could sign a legally binding cooperation contract. Agreements would be reached through negotiations among involved parties. The third stage would be characterized by friendly goodwill. Every interested party in the region should move beyond dependence on contract terms and will have a deep understanding of the implications of cross-regional collaboration. This is essential for recognizing the overall benefits of the Beijing-Tianjin-Hebei metropolitan area.

Moreover, the metropolitan area should build a multi-collaborative governance mechanism to improve the performance of the Beijing-Tianjin-Hebei metropolitan collaborative network. For the past three decades, the practice of multi-collaborative governance driven by non-governmental organizations, enterprises and regional cooperative organizations has been flourishing. Due to the lack of a department responsible for regional policy implementation in the Beijing-Tianjin-Hebei metropolitan area, it is necessary to establish a cross-jurisdiction collaborative organization. This organization could be endowed by the central government with the authority to allocate funds and manage public affairs in the metropolitan area. It could also establish various special funds for different types of regional collaborative governance. These funds would mainly be provided by the central government, local governments in the metropolitan area, various foundations and donations from private sectors. This measure could help offset the cost of communication and negotiation between collaborative members in the region. In addition, it would be an effective motivator, encouraging non-governmental organizations, enterprises and citizens to participate in regional affairs.

Finally, the metropolitan area should build an interest distribution and compensation mechanism in the collaborative network to achieve regional coordinated development. During and after the process of collaboration, a conflict of interest among the various parties might emerge. Therefore, it is necessary to establish a compensation and coordination mechanism composed of central government and cross-jurisdiction collaborative organizations during the integration of the Beijing-Tianjin-Hebei metropolitan area. Although water supply and water environmental safety in Beijing and

Tianjin are guaranteed, some regions in Hebei Province have faced a series of ecological and environmental problems for a long time, such as the demand for water exceeding supply, soil erosion and water pollution. These problems, together with the poverty belt in Hebei Province which surrounding Beijing and Tianjin, make ecological and environmental compensations in the Beijing-Tianjin-Hebei collaborative network very important.[26] Therefore, cities in Hebei Province could submit an application to the cross-jurisdiction collaborative organization, which could offer reasonable compensation after an assessment. If there is a dispute between the cooperating parties regarding the amount of compensation, the central government could readjust the funds. In addition, Beijing and Tianjin, as the core cities in the area, should give certain benefits to other local governments during the integration of the metropolitan area in order to achieve the maximum overall benefit to the region.

This study is not without limitations. First, the applied collaborative network data are mainly about public affairs such as health, transportation, law enforcement and environmental issues, but we do not analyze different types of collaborative networks in respective fields. However, for the metropolitan areas of developing countries, observing different types of collaborative networks does not reflect the overall collaboration status of this metropolitan area due to the low level of collaborations in respective fields. For these reasons, we have chosen collaboration data of some typical public affairs regardless of their respective fields. Second, this chapter discusses only one metropolitan area, which limits the breath of applicability of research results.

Despite these limitations, this chapter might provide some useful information for the study of metropolitan governance. As the collaborative development of the Beijing-Tianjin-Hebei metropolitan area is an important national strategy for China, its collaborative governance can serve as a useful reference for the metropolitan governance of developing countries.

## Notes

1 LeRoux, Kelly, Paul W. Brandenburger and Sanjay K. Pandey, "Interlocal Service Cooperation in U.S. Cities: A Social Network Explanation," *Public Administration Review* 70 (2): 268–270.
2 Savitch, H. V. and Ronald K. Vogel, "Paths to New Regionalism," *State and Local Government Review* 32 (3): 158–168; Wallis, Allan D., "The Third Wave: Current Trends in Regional Governance," *National Civic Review* 1994 (Summer–Fall): 290–310.
3 Feiock, Richard C., *Metropolitan Governance: Conflict, Competition, and Cooperation* (Washington, D.C.: Georgetown University Press, 2004).

4 Feiock, Richard C. and John T. Scholz, *Self-Organizing Federalism: Collabo-rative Mechanisms to Mitigate Institutional Collective Action Dilemmas* (New York: Cambridge University Press, 2010).

5 Wasserman, Stanley and Katherine Faust, *Social Network Analysis: Methods and Application* (Cambridge: Cambridge University Press, 1994).

6 Peter De Leon, Danielle M. Varda, "Toward a Theory of Collaborative Policy Networks: Identifying Structural Tendencies," *Policy Studies Journal* 37 (1): 59–74.

7 Robert Agranoff and Michael McGuire, "Big Questions in Public Network Management Research," *Journal of Public Administration Research and Theory* 11 (3): 295–326; O'Toole Laurence J., Jr., "Treating Networks Seri-ously: Practical and Research-Based Agendas in Public Administration," *Public Administration Review* 57 (1): 45–52; John M. Bryson, Barbara C. Crosby and Melissa Middleton Stone, "The Design and Implementation of Cross-Sector Collaborations: Propositions from the Literature," *Public Admin-istration Review* 66 (S1): 44–55.

8 B. Chen and J. Krauskopf, "Integrated or Disconnected? Examining Formal and Informal Networks in a Merged Nonprofit Organization," *Nonprofit Man-agement & Leadership* 23 (3): 325–345.

9 Stephanie S. Post, "Metropolitan Area Governance and Institutional Collective Action," in Richard C. Feiock (ed.) *Metropolitan Governance: Conflict, Com-petition, and Cooperation* (Washington, D.C.: Georgetown University Press, 2004), 67–92.

10 Ronald J. Oakerson, *Governing Local Public Economics: Creating the Civic Metropolis* (Oakland: ICS Press, 1999); Ronald J. Oakerson, "The Study of Metropolitan Governance," in Richard C. Feiock (ed.) *Metropolitan Govern-ance: Conflict, Competition, and Cooperation* (Washington, D.C.: Georgetown University Press, 2004).

11 Allan D. Wallis, "The Third Wave: Current Trends in Regional Governance," *National Civic Review* 1994 (Summer–Fall): 290–310.

12 Lin Ye, "Regional Government and Governance in China and the United States," *Public Administration Review* December 2009: S116–S121.

13 Richard C. Feiock and John T. Scholz, *Self-Organizing Federalism: Collabo-rative Mechanisms to Mitigate Institutional Collective Action Dilemmas* (New York: Cambridge University Press, 2010).

14 Kelly LeRoux, Paul W. Brandenburger, Sanjay K. Pandey, "Interlocal Service Cooperation in U.S. Cities: A Social Network Explanation," *Public Adminis-tration Review* 70 (2): 268–270.

15 Annette Steinacker, "Game-Theoretic Models of Metropolitan Cooperation," in Richard C. Feiock (ed.) *Metropolitan Governance: Conflict, Competition, and Cooperation* (Washington, D.C.: Georgetown University Press, 2004), 46–66.

16 Richard H. Thaler, "Anomalies: The Ultimatum Game," *Journal of Economic Perspectives* 2 (4): 95–206.

17 Qing Shu and Keyu Zhou, *From Closed to Open: The Analysis of Administrative Area Economy in China*, (Shanghai: East China Normal University Press, 2003).

18 Long Yang and Yanqiang Peng, "The Study on the Local Government Cooperation in China from the Perspective of the Assignment of Administra-tive Jurisdiction," *Journal of Political Science* 2009 (4): 61–64.

19 Aiping Yang, "From Vertical Incentives to Horizontal Incentives: the Innova-tion of Interest Motivation Mechanism of Local Government Collaboration,"

*Academic Research* 2011 (5): 47–53; Gangqiang Yu and Lihui Cai, "The Study on the Network Governance Patterns of the Metropolitan in China," *Chinese Public Administration* 2011 (6): 96.

20  Taijun Jin and Yuqing Tang, "The Dilemma of the Collaborative Governance of Regional Ecology and its Solutions," *Journal of Nanjing Normal University (Social Science Edition)* 2011 (5): 17–21.

21  Jing Cui, "The Study on the Holistic Governance of the Cross-Jurisdiction Public Affairs: A Case Study of the Beijing-Tianjin-Hebei Metropolitan in China," *Journal of Political Science* 2012 (2): 92.

22  Xu Zhang, Xiaorui Zhang, "The Win-win Integration of the Capital Economic Circle Driving on the Fast Track," *Beijing News*, 2011: B04.

23  Xiushan Chen and Yan Yang, "The Evolution of Regional Development Strategy and the Target Selection on Regional Collaborative Development in China," *Teaching and Research* 2008 (5): 5–6.

24  Jing Cui, "Interlocal Collaboration and Integration: The Study on the Operation Mode of cross-Jurisdiction Public Affairs in the Metropolitan," *Reform* 2011 (7): 84–85.

25  Jing Cui, "Interlocal Collaboration and Integration: The Study on the Operation Mode of cross-Jurisdiction Public Affairs in the Metropolitan," *Reform* 2011 (7): 84–85.

26  Research Team of Poverty Belt Surrounding Beijing and Tianjin. *Annual Report on China's Regional Economy (2009–2010)*, edited by Qi Benchao and Jing Tihua (Beijing: Social Science Academic Press, 2010), 176–177.

# 6    Conclusion

Along with the advance of regional integration, collaborative governance in metropolitan areas such as the Yangtze River Delta, the Pearl River Delta and the Beijing-Tianjin-Hebei region, has attracted more and more attention. Recently, the coordinated development of Beijing and Tianjin has been elevated to the national strategic level, which provides a new opportunity for the development of Beijing-Tianjin-Hebei metropolitan area. Hence, research on collaborative governance in metropolitan areas appears to be essential and important. However, owning to the continuous emergence of administration division or fragmentation in regional governance, uneven development of collaborative members in economy, society and environment, the absence of cross-boundary administrative coordination agents, as well as the imperfect trust mechanism, benefit distribution mechanism and evaluation mechanism, it is difficult to achieve long-term effective collaboration between local governments in metropolitan area. As a result, collaborative governance in metropolitan area becomes a topic which has yet to be further researched both in theory and practice.

Holistic governance, as a new approach of governance after new public management, whose application in regional collaborative governance is becoming an emerging research field of public management. The theory of holistic governance, which is stemming from "holism," characterized by collaboration, integration and "cross-domain," focusing on the overall interests, and emphasizing that when dealing with public affairs, governments should not only integrate the internal agents and functions, but also promote the collaboration among governments, private sectors and non-profit organizations, so as to formulate a holistic governance network. So, local government's collaboration in metropolitan governance has some internal relations with the theory of holistic governance. The theoretical framework of local government's holistic collaborative governance in metropolitan areas adopted in this study, as well as the mechanism and mode of holistic collaborative governance based on it, provide a theoretical support for the diagnosis and optimization of collaborative governance of cross-boundary public affairs in metropolitan area. In terms of research methods, besides traditional literature analysis, investigations including interview methods and case studies, social network analysis (SNA) are also used to analyze the collaborative governance in metropolitan areas. This makes a visualization measurement of relational data that is difficult to be quantified. This study uses it as a methodological support for empirical analysis of collaborative governance network in metropolitan area, thus, the structure and performance of such network can be analyzed step by step on the basis of density, degree centrality and between centrality.

With regional spatial reorganization, local governments of metropolitan area in China have experienced the changes from competition to cooperation, from simple cooperation in economic and technology to metropolitan planning and to primary public affairs collaboration. After more than 30 years' effort, local governments have formed rudimentary forms of collaboration, such as cooperation and communication, signing intergovernmental cooperation agreements, and the inter-regional counterpart support. However, due to the diverse preferences in policy objectives of local governments, the asymmetry of local government's strength and the political tournament model for local official's promotion, collaboration between local governments in metropolitan area is restricted. In this sense, it is necessary to construct the mechanism and mode of holistic collaboration governance of local governments in metropolitan area.

The mechanism of holistic collaboration governance among local governments in metropolitan area consists of the mechanisms of trust and communication, interest distribution and compensation, supervision and evaluation. In detail, the establishment of trust and communication mechanism needs to go through three stages, that is, a careful trial phase to construct dialogue and communication channels, a phase of signing agreements to reconcile contradictions and conflicts, and a phase of promoting mutual understanding and trust. The construction of interests distribution and compensation mechanism needs to coordinate the interest relationship between local governments, under the direction and supervision of central governments and regional high-level governments, besides establishing the vertical transfer payment mechanisms, horizontal transfer payment mode, private trading and market trading mechanisms, public participation mechanism, and Eco-labeling and NGO participation mechanisms, which is to ensure the smooth and orderly cooperation between metropolitan governments. Supervision and evaluation system shall consist of horizontal monitoring and evaluation mechanism between local governments in metropolitan area, vertical monitoring and evaluation mechanism between central and local governments, and third-party supervision and evaluation mechanism.

To establish the mode of holistic collaboration governance among local governments in metropolitan area, four aspects need to be established and improved, that is, the information platform and the integration of collaborative governance system, the inter-regional holistic collaborative organization, holistic collaboration governance mechanism and the holistic collaborative governance network in metropolitan area. More precisely, what needs in constructing a regional information sharing and communicating platform is to create an information support system in cross-border regional governance, cross-boundary mechanisms for information integration and information service, thus constituting a united regional system of personnel administration, fiscal expenditure and information network. As an important organizational form in metropolitan holistic governance, cross-boundary holistic collaborative organization, with its own legitimacy and authority, holds the financial distribution and management rights for the special funds in dealing with the cross-border public affairs in metropolitan area. Based on the holistic collaborative governance mechanism, the collaborative network that consists of government at the higher level (the central government), local government in metropolitan area, private sectors, NGOs and cross-border collaborative organizations, is an important way to attain regional holistic governance.

Based on a theoretical study on holistic governance mechanism and model of local governments in metropolitan area, by using the Social Network Analysis (SNA) to analyze the collaboration among 13 local governments in Beijing-Tianjin-Hebei Metropolitan Area, this book reveals that the network density of Beijing-Tianjin-Hebei Metropolitan Area is not high but the relationship among members in this network is becoming closer and closer overtime. Comparatively, as two core cities, Beijing and Tianjin are more prominent nodes although their networks' development is restricted by other cities in the metropolitan area. While Chengde, Baoding, Langfang and Zhangjiakou play the "broker" roles in this collaboration network, actively connect with Beijing and Tianjin with geographical advantages, in order to accept spillovers and become an emerging condensing subgroup. However, more extensive networks have yet to formulate and the synergy effect in the network is not obvious. Therefore, for more extensive collaboration, better mechanisms for communication, compensation and trust building need to be in place.

Through a case study of air pollution collaborative governance in the Beijing-Tianjin-Hebei Metropolitan Area, we can find that the authority of central and local governments in China's metropolitan governance can be divided in line with the attributes of public goods. Central governments are primarily responsible for setting national standards for the emission of major pollutants on the one hand, and one the other hand, they also take charge of the coordination and compensation of trans-boundary pollution control. While the governments of provinces, autonomous regions and municipalities directly under the central government shall make implementation plans for curbing air pollution within the region, and control cross-regional pollutants with other provinces and cities. Larger municipal governments should adjust emission standards and implement pollution plans, with the authorization of central governments and the provincial government. And country or district governments are held accountable for the implementations. In the meanwhile, central governments should grant partial rights to local governments for environmental jurisdiction, but still need to avoid the effect of "environmental race to the bottom" and "environmental race to the top," so as to strengthen the guiding role in pollution control. Regional air pollution governance requires transferring rights between local governments and constructing cross-regional collaborative organizations. Through cross-boundary collaborative organizations, local governments can jointly govern regional public affairs by setting up mutual funds, signing cooperation agreement, and involving private sectors and non-profit organizations.

Finally, through a case of NIMBY protests in the process of urbanization in China, we can examine the relationship between local government and civil society in the process of metropolitan areas moving forward regional governance.

In the face of the neighborhood facilities, "organizational irresponsibility" makes people in some regions bear a huge risk, while the way of people expressing their demands is limited to some extent. As a "sub politics" and "new social movement," the NIMBY becomes the main way for people in social learning and gaining experience on collective actions. In decision-making of NIMBY policy, improving communication and exchange of risk information is very important to enhance the public's understanding of risk issues as well as their trust and confidence in the governments. Conflicts between governments and the public over NIMBY will be largely alleviated or solved when the governments expand public participation in decision-making process of NIMBY policy, trust the public's judgment and scientific knowledge, and bear more responsibility for information disclosure, eliminating threats, and health protection. Today, in an increasing complicated and dangerous environment, the negotiation mechanism among various shareholders such as local governments, the public and NGOs will facilitate regional governance.

In conclusion, in the process of achieving long-term, stable, effective collaborations and regional governance in China's metropolitan area, we can improve the regional governance performance from the following aspects:

## Reinforcement of the intergovernmental collaboration

Holistic governance in metropolitan area cannot do without the coordination of intergovernmental relations and the division of intergovernmental jurisdiction. Whether the relationship between central government and local government, and between local government and local government is coordinated or not directly affects the performance of collaborative governance of metropolitan area. Paul R. Dommel argues that intergovernmental relations have evolved from the delineation of powers between the state and local governments to a highly complicated system of shared responsibility and problem solving.[1] Hence, in holistic governance of metropolitan area, the first thing that needs to be coordinated is the relationships between central and local governments, second is the relationships among local governments in metropolitan area. Specifically, it reflects in the following aspects:

### *The central government should promulgate policies and regulations supporting metropolitan collaboration, to guide and fund the development of the metropolitan area*

In the process of rapid development of China's metropolitan area or urban agglomeration, it is urgent for the central government to issue a serious of policies and regulations for coordinating the collaboration of local governments in metropolitan area, supporting regional industrial development, and revolving economic disputes in the cooperation. On the one hand, regional contract observed by the local governments in metropolitan area should be formulated, which is used to constrain local government's behavior and urge them to take collective actions. At the same time, based on these policies and regulations, central governments need to coordinate the interests of various local governments in metropolitan area, and allocate special funds for the governance of cross-regional public affairs through vertical transfer payments. For example, in environmental governance of metropolitan area, in order to alleviate the shortage of transfer payments for ecological environment protection, local governments in China's metropolitan area can explore ways to obtain funds in the form of ecological tax and environmental tax, which requires the central government to issue relevant laws and regulations to provide legal basis for the establishment of ecological tax or environmental tax. For another example, to adopt the private trade and market trade mechanism to carry out regional ecological compensation, we need to establish a market-oriented trading mechanism of water rights and emission rights, but the establishment of such mechanism needs to define China's water rights and emission rights in law, establish the emission permit system, and make the emission permit become a scarce resource that can be traded in the market, which also needs relevant laws and regulations.

### *Improving the local official's performance appraisal system and promoting the transfer and balance of power between local governments*

In the current GDP-led promotion mechanism of officials in China, local officials in local affairs management will consider more about their relative position with competitors in promotion, while they are not keen on regional public affairs collaborative governance. Therefore, it is necessary to reform the existing assessment system for local officials, that is, no longer taking the GDP of local governments as the main assessment index of official performance, but should incorporate the indicators such as "regional cooperation performance" and "environmental protection" into performance appraisal system as the important assessment index of local officials. Only in this way can the local governments participate in regional governance. At the same time, the imbalance of status and influence among different local governments in the metropolitan area also hinders the realization of collaborative governance. So, the central government should balance the interests of local governments, encourage local governments to provide public goods or services with positive spillover effects, and reduce negative spillover effects between local governments, so as to avoid the situation of "beggar-thy-neighbor" and the phenomena of "interrupted roads" and "interrupted bridges." Furthermore, through the transfer of administrative jurisdiction between local governments in metropolitan area, a cross-boundary regional common authority beyond the local authority is formed, which can be exercised by a cross-regional holistic organization. The transfer of power enables local governments to reach a certain balance in the governance of regional public affairs, and effectively coordinate the actions between local governments in metropolitan area.

### The establishment of a unified information network system in metropolitan area

The governance of metropolitan area in the digital era should focus on the re-integration of public services and emphasize the overall and collaborative decision-making mode. To realize the integrated governance of the metropolitan area, it is necessary to establish a developed information network support system, form a unified personnel administration, financial expenditure and information network system in the region, and realize the information sharing of talents, science and technology, and commerce.

In order to build a unified information network system in the metropolitan area, it is necessary for local governments in the metropolitan area to implement the integration of internal institutions and functions in accordance with the principle of functional correspondence, so as to form a unified personnel administration, financial expenditure and information network system in the region. The functional departments of local governments in the region cooperate directly with the functional departments of cross-regional holistic collaboration organizations to solve cross-boundary public problems. What is more, it is better to set up a regional information sharing platform to connect government websites of local governments and its relevant departments to achieve information networking and timely exchange of related policies. As a result, all departments can release information and share it in real time on the same platform, realizing rapid communication between local governments and breaking down the barriers between governments and departments.

Second, an information support system for cross-regional governance should be established to link databases resources of various local governments, providing information and data support for local governments in metropolitan area and private sectors and non-profit organizations involved in regional governance. Furthermore, the construction of a cross-boundary information integration mechanism has an important role in information integration and unification on regional important issues for cooperation, such as collaborative governance in regional air pollution control, emergency rescue cooperation in cross-boundary public crisis events, holistic collaboration of water resources within the region, as well as transportation and land planning, so as to improve regional overall information level.

Finally, it is necessary to break down the regional and departmental barriers, and establish an open, unified and transparent capital market as well as the factor market. In addition, a cross-regional information service mechanism should be established to provide comprehensive and convenient information services to enterprises and the public by the form of portal websites for policy regulations and information, such as local government affairs, economic trade and public services. Moreover, it is necessary to promote the equalization of basic public services, realize the accessibility and convenience of people's access to regional infrastructure and basic public services, such as remote settlement of endowment insurance, and contribute to regional integration of technology, finance, accounting, legal advice, logistics and talents.

## Establishing cross-jurisdiction holistic collaborative organization in metropolitan area

In the collaborative governance of China's metropolitan area, it is imperative to construct cross-jurisdiction holistic collaborative organization. Under the current system, it is more feasible to establish a cross-jurisdiction collaborative organization with the participation of all local governments in metropolitan area to coordinate the regional development plan, led by the central government. Such organizations may be government agencies, independent legal entities or NGOs. There are three main sources of funding for cross-jurisdiction holistic collaborative organization: financial support from regional governments, financial allocation from central governments or the governments at the next higher level, and donation of the foundations and the private sector. The cross-jurisdiction holistic collaborative organization should be endowed by the central government with the right of financial distribution and supervision over the cross-regional public affairs, to ensure the legitimacy and authority of the collaborative organization itself, which then makes sure that the overall regional policies are implemented and enforced effectively.

The establishment of a cross-jurisdiction cooperative organization in the metropolitan area should follow the voluntary principle. It is composed of various local governments in metropolitan area voluntarily, to ensure that all local governments can voluntarily join and withdraw the organization, so as to enhance the trust of all local governments in the cooperation organization. In addition, cross-jurisdiction holistic collaborative organization may consist of local officials, NPC (National People's Congress) members, experts and scholars who come from metropolitan area. Moreover, representatives of local governments in metropolitan area should maintain the same number, so as to assure a fair distribution of benefits in cross-boundary holistic cooperative organization and fully guarantee the fair rights and interests of each participant. There are three main functions of cross-jurisdiction holistic collaborative organizations in metropolitan area:

### *The formulation of a regional development plan for entire metropolitan area and the coordination of functional positioning and industrial division for local governments*

The cross-jurisdiction collaborative organizations are responsible for formulating guidelines and policies for the overall development of metropolitan areas, striving for regional development projects and policies from the state, and providing information and suggestions to regional economic development and social management for regional governments, especially for local government's functional positioning and division of labor within the region. In the functional positioning, there is a need for cross-jurisdiction holistic organizations to coordinate the functional positioning of local governments in metropolitan area with the central government. For example, some scholars suggest that Beijing should be positioned on the "capital function" in Beijing-Tianjin-Hebei Metropolitan, establish "capital public finance" for separate budget and expenditures so that they can no longer participate in competition for investment attraction within the region, which may avoid vicious competition among local governments within metropolitan areas.[2] According to industrial division of labor, which adapts to the functional positioning, there are varying degrees of industrial integration and redundant infrastructure in China's metropolitan areas. For instance, due to lack of unified coordination and planning, various cities in the Yangtze River Delta are building airports one after another. As a result, high-density airports construction is far beyond the limited demands of local passengers and goods transportation. For this, it is necessary to coordinate and adjust the industrial layout and industrial transfer of each local government on the basis of functional positioning, taking both economically developed areas and backward areas into consideration, as well as the development of ecological water sources and receiving place, in order to achieve inclusive development in the whole metropolitan area.

### *The allocation of regional special funds among local governments in metropolitan area*

Funds from central governments or higher-level governments in trans-boundary public affairs governance, fiscal support from various local governments in the region, as well as donation from foundations and the private sectors need to be allocated. Funds for regional environmental protection, housing, transportation, water resource distribution and other aspects must be allocated by cross-jurisdiction collaborative organizations to local governments involved in the holistic collaborative organization, while non-membership local governments have no right to obtain such funds.

### *The establishment of a special committee under collaborative organizations for interest coordination and compensation between local governments in metropolitan area*

Special committees can be set up in areas such as regional water resources allocation, air pollution control, infrastructure and social undertaking, with the responsibilities for special governance funds that used to different types of regional collaborative governance. Especially in ecology and environment, it is urgent to establish a special committee under cross-jurisdiction holistic collaborative organization to coordinate the interests and compensation of various actors. In metropolitan governance, local governments with serious losses of interests can submit an application to a special committee of cross-jurisdiction holistic collaborative organizations for benefits compensation, then, based on loss assessments, special committee may use special funds to compensate ecological damage and environmental pollution. If the two or more parties have disputes over the loss of benefits, the higher-level government of the region, such as the central government or the provincial government can intervene and mediate it, as well as organize collaborative parties, the private sectors, foundations and other relevant institutions to donate the part that the special fund is not enough to compensate.

Central cities like Beijing, Shanghai and some provincial capital cities with the support of surrounding local governments in the development process are taking the lead in economic and social development. Therefore, in the process of metropolitan collaboration, these central cities need to transfer their interests to other local governments in an inclusive manner to maximize the overall interests of the region.

## The construction of multigovernance mechanism of local government's collaborative governance in metropolitan area

The multi governance mechanism is where local governments in metropolitan area absorb various kinds of non-governmental organizations, private departments, citizens and regional cooperation organizations to take part in regional holistic governance, relying on flexible horizontal governance network to enhance collaborative development. In regional governance and urban governance, regional local government have mobilized the initiatives of all kinds of social organizations, enterprises and regional collaborative organizations and introduces multi governance, which is a new governance model that has flourished in the world in the last 20 to 30 years.

As mentioned above, new regionalism advocates that local governments should absorb non-profit organizations, the private sector and the public in regional governance, and establish regional collaborative organizations, with a flexible horizontal governance network rather than simple government management, so as to integrate and coordinate regional development. In Canada, for example, such multi collaborative governance network has been set up for the management of the St. Lawrence river basin. Led by the Environment Ministry, with the participation from departments of agriculture, maritime and fisheries, and economic development, a management system of unified watershed planning, sub-sector implementation, supervision and inspection by law enforcement departments is formed. It also actively encourages enterprise and community residents to get involved in river basin pollution control, and set up the St. Lawrence river management center to carry out environmental monitor and information exchange.[3] Building cross-sector partnerships is to create a governance structure for collaboration among the public sector, private sector and the third department, and form new synergies to solve the increasingly complex regional public issues based on collaborative governance structure.[4] In the practice of foreign countries, this kind of cooperation often forms regional alliance or urban alliance, which links the diverse interest subjects together, realizes the cooperation between the public and private sectors, and thus carries out some policies or reforms. The Pittsburgh Regional Alliance, established in Pittsburgh, USA, is a trans-Pittsburgh urban union based principally on the private sector (commercial chamber) and second on the public sector, which aims to promote trans-regional social participation and government cooperation.[5]

In the practice of regional cooperation in China, the multi governance mechanism has not been established and non-profit organizations, the private sectors as well as citizens are not entirely engaged in regional public affairs. After the reform and opening up, various local governments in China, around the center of "economic construction," and in order to promote local economic growth and maximize its own interests, various local governments in China have formed different types of interest alliances with many economic development subjects in cities, forming a complex and powerful "urban growth alliance."[6] This kind of alliance is the combination of the strong desire of local officials to develop local economy and the motive of business elites to gather wealth, and it is also the combination of political elites and economic elites in the city.[7] The most typical representative one is the "growth coalition" created by local governments and real estate enterprises in the process of China economic progress.[8] Due to the excessive attention to economic growth or GDP, there is more competition between local governments than cooperation, and cooperation is restricted to the economy field.

Recently, some scholars believe that regional cooperation in the Yangtze River Delta has obvious characteristics of new regionalism.[9] Among them, the Yangtze River Delta Urban Economic Coordination Council plays a major role in economic cooperation, which takes enterprises as the main participants and introduces social intermediary organizations such as associations and chambers, to promote the process of regional integration together. Multiple collaboration management alliance is also emerged within the city. For instance, the joint governance model of Hangzhou's social composite subjects reflects the trend from the government's single pole governance to the joint governance of multiple social subjects. Hangzhou's "social composite subject includes government departments, knowledge groups, industrial and mass media departments." The role of social composite subjects in coordination, regulation, development and operation of urban public affairs is shown in projects of Hangzhou Canal, Remodeling of the courtyard, the West Lake Exposition, Tea alliance strategic association, and the Silk and Women's Wear Industry Alliance. Those cross-sectional consortium, in compliance with the division of labors, take collective actions for their common interests.[10] Led by the governments, multiple agents formed a cross-sectional social composite agent, which reconstructed a cross-section governance structure through synthesizing resources from the administrative department, the market and the society, and also formed an organizational running system for which multiple agents were jointly responsible.[11] In conclusion, multi governance mechanism of local government collaborative governance in metropolitan area is mainly to establish an all-around partnership of collaboration among local governments, enterprises and non-profit organizations in order to achieve collaborative governance in the aspects of public service, infrastructure construction, public crisis, the private sector and NGO can complement part of government public management functions, thus become a way for them to participate in social governance.

## Notes

1 Paul R. Dommel, "Intergovernmental Relations," in Richard D. Bingham (ed.), *Management Local Government: Public Administration in Practice* (Beijing: Peking University Press, 1997), 166–177.
2 Yang Lianyun, Shi Yabi. "Jingjinyiquyuxietiaofazhan de zhanluesikao" ["The Strategic Thinking of Harmonious Development of Beijing, Tianjin, and Hebei"]. *Hebei xueken* [*Hebei Academic Journal*] Vol. 4 (2006).
3 Hu Yi, Chen Ruilian, "Fadaguojia de liuyushuiwurangonggongzhilijizhijiqiqishi" ["Public Governance Mechanism of River Basin Pollution in Developed Country and Its Enlightenment"]. *Tianjin xingzhengxueyuanxuebao* [*Journal of Tianjin Administration Institute*] Vol. 1 (2006).
4 Zhang Jingen, "Fuji zhili: dangdai zhongguo fujiguanxi yanjiu de xinquxiang" ["Intergovernmental Governance: The New Trend for Research on Intergovernmental Relations in Current China"]. *Xueshuyanjiu* [*Academic Research*] Vol. 2 (2013).
5 Cai He, "Cong tongzhidaozhili: zhongguochengshihuaguochengzhong de dachengshishehuiguanli" ["From Government to Governance: The Social Management in Chinese Urban during the Process of Urbanization"]. *Gonggongxingzhengpinglun* [*Journal of Public Administration Review*] Vol. 6 (2012).

6 Growth machine is also called pro-growth coalitions, the theory acknowledges that entrepreneurial activism is the main force sharing urban systems, urban development is a product of growth coalition, and participants in the coalition include economic interest groups (such as land developers, builders, financiers), leaders of the public and the third sectors, and organizations with indirect interests in urban development (local media, retailers, services). See John R. Logan and Harvey L. Molotch, *Urban Fortunes: The Political Economy of Place* (Berkeley: University of California Press, 1987): 53–65 and Tingwei Zhang, "Urban Development and a Socialist Pro-growth Coalition in Shanghai," *Urban Affairs Review*, Vol. 37, No. 4, (2002).

7 Harvey L. Molotch, "The City as a Growth Machine," *The American Journal of Sociology*, Vol. 82, No. 2, (1976).

8 Zhang Zhenhua, "Zengzhanglianmeng: fenxizhuanxingqiwoguo defang zhengfuyuliyijituanguanxi de yizhonglilun shijiao" ["Growth Coalition: A Theoretical Perspective to Analyze the Relation Between Local Government and Economic Interest Group in China's Transitional Period"]. *Tianjin shehuikexue* [*Tianjin Social Sciences*] Vol. 1 (2011).

9 Ye Lin, "Xinquyuzhuyi de xingqiyufazhan: yigezongshu" ["A Review of Literature on New Regionalism"]. *Gonggongxingzhengpinglun* [*Journal of Public Administration Review*] Vol. 3 (2010).

10 Linka, Liyong, Shenqiu, "Shehuiguanlichuangxin he tuijinduoyuanzhutifazhan de hangzhoujingyanyanjiu" ["Study on the Hangzhou Experience of Social Management Innovation and the Promotion of Multiple Social Subjects' Development"]. *Shehuikexuezhanxian* [*Social Science Frontier*] Vol. 3 (2013).

11 Zhang Zhaishu, "Chengshiyitiyushehuifuhezhuti de lianhezhili: dui Hangzhou sanZhong chengshizhilishijian de zuzhifenxi" ["Urban Issues and Social Multiple Agents' Joint Governance"]. *Guanlishijie* [*Management World*] Vol. 2 (2012).

# Bibliography

Agranoff, Robert and Michael McGuire. "Big Questions in Public Network Management Research." *Journal of Public Administration Research and Theory,* vol. 11, no. 3 (2010): 295–326.

Alter, Catherine and Jerald Hage, *Organizations Working Together.* Newbury Park, CA: Sage Publications, 1993.

Bish, Robert L. and Vincent Ostrom, *Understanding Urban Government: Metropolitan Reform Reconsidered,* Washington, D.C: American Enterprise Institute, 1973.

Bo Guili, *Jiquanfenquanyuguojia de xingshuai* [*Centralization and Decentralization and the Rise and Fall of the Country*]. Beijing: jingjikexuechubanshe [Beijing: Economic Science Press], 2001.

Bryson, John M., Barbara C. Crosby and Melissa Middleton Stone. "The Design and Implementation of Cross-Sector Collaborations: Propositions from the Literature." *Public Administration Review,* vol. 66 (S1) (2006): 44–55.

Cai He. "Cong tongzhidaozhili: zhongguochengshihuaguochengzhong de dachengshishehuiguanli" ["From Government to Governance: The Social Management in Chinese Urban during the Process of Urbanization"]. *Gonggongxingzhengpinglun* [*Journal of Public Administration Review*], vol. 6 (2012).

Chen Lie, Sun Haijun, Zhang Surong. "Jiyuditanjingji de huanjingjinpinkundaifazhanmoshiyanjiu" ["Research on Development Model of the Poverty Belt around Beijing and Tianjin Based on Low Carbon Economy"]. *Fazhanyanjiu* [*Development Research*], vol. 6 (2012).

Chen Ruilian et al., *Study on Theory and Practice of Regional Public Management.* Beijing, China Social Science Press, 2008.

Chen Ruilian, Kong Kai. "Zhongguoquyugonggongguanliyanjiu de fazhanyuqianzhan" ["Development and Prospect of Regional Public Management Research in China"]. *Xueshuyanjiu* [*Academic Research*], vol. 5 (2009): 45–49.

Chen Ruilian, Liu Yaping, et al. *Regional Governance Research: A Perspective of International Comparison.* Beijing: Central Compilation and Translation Press, 2013.

Chen Ruilian, Liu Yaping. "Fan zhusanjiaoquyuzhengfu de hezuoyuchuangxin" ["Cooperation and Innovation of the Pan-Pearl River Delta Regional Government"]. *Xueshuyanjiu* [*Academic Research*], vol. 1 (2007): 42–50.

Chen Ruilian, Rengmin, *Zhongguoliuyuzhiliyanjiubaogao* [*Research Report of River Basin Governance in China*]. Shanghai: Gezhichubanshe [Shanghai: Truth and Wisdom Press], 2011: 242.

Chen Ruilian, Yang Aiping. "Cong quyugonggongguanlidaoquyuzhiliyanjiu: lishi de zhuanxing" ["The Historical Transformation from Regional Public Management to Regional Governance"]. *Nankaixuebao (zhexueshehuikexue ban)* [*Nankai Journal. Philosophy, Literature and Social Science Edition*], vol. 2 (2012): 48–57.

Chen Ruilian, *Quyugonggongguanlililunyushijianyanjiu* ["Research on Theory and Practice of Regional Public Management"]. Beijing: Zhongguoshehuikexuechubanshe [*Chinese Social Science Press*], 2008.

Chen Ruilian. "Lunquyugonggongguanliyanjiu de yuanqiyufazhan" ["Research on the Origin and Development of Regional Public Management"]. *Zhengzhixueyanjiu* [*Cass Journal of Political Science*], vol. 4 (2003): 75–84.

Chen Shengyong, Ma Bin. "Quyujianzhengfuhezuo: quyujingjiyitihua de lujingxuanze" ["Inter-regional government cooperation: the path choice of regional economic integration"]. *Zhengzhixueyanjiu* [*Cass Journal of Political Science*], vol. 1 (2004): 24–34.

Chen, B., and J. Krauskopf. "Integrated or Disconnected? Examining Formal and Informal Networks in a Merged Nonprofit Organization". *Nonprofit Management & Leadership*, 2013, vol 23, no. 3: 325–345.

Chen, Xiushan, and Yan Yang. "The Evolution of Regional Development Strategy and the Target Selection on Regional Collaborative Development in China". *Teaching and Research*, vol. 5 (2008): 5–6.

Chu Dajian, Li Zhongzheng. "Wangluozhilishijiaoxia de gonggongfuwuzhenghechutan" ["Probe into the Integration of Public Service from the Perspective of Network Governance"]. *Zhongguoxingzhengguanli* [*Chinese Public Administration*], vol. 8 (2007): 34–36.

Chu Dajian. "Shanghai yuchangsanjiaoquyuxietiaofazhanzhong de wentisikao" ["Thinking on the Problems of the Coordinated Development Between Shanghai and Yangtze River Delta Region"]. *Shanghai chengshiguihua* [*Shanghai Urban Planning Review*], vol. 2 (2011): 7–9.

COG Mission, *Metropolitan Washington Council of Government*. www.mwcog.org/community/planning-areas/regional-planning/, accessed on December 30, 2019.

Cui Jing. "Shengtaizhilizhong de difangzhengfu xiezuo: zi jingjinyiiquan guancha" ["The Collaboration of Local Government on Ecological Governance: from the Prospect of the Metropolitan Area of Beijing-Tianjin-Hebei"]. *Gaige* [*Reform*], vol. 9 (2013).

Cui Jing. "Dadushiqukuajiegonggongshiwuyunxingmoshi: fujixiezuoyuzhenghe" ["The Operational Mode of Metropolitan Cross-jurisdiction Public Affairs: The Cooperation and Integration Between Government"]. *Gaige* [*Reform*], vol. 7 (2011): 82–87.

Cui Jing. "Quyudifangzhengfukuajiagonggongshiwuzhengtixingzhilimoshiyanjiu: yijingjinjidushiquanweili" ["A Study on the Overall Governance Model of Regional Local Governments' Cross-border Public Affairs Taking the Beijing-

Tianjin-Hebei Metropolitan Area as an Example"]. *Zhengzhixueyanjiu* [*CASS Journal of Political Science*], vol. 2 (2012): 91–97.

Cui Jing. "Interlocal Collaboration and Integration: The Study on the Operation Mode of cross-Jurisdiction Public Affairs in the Metropolitan". *Reform*, vol 7 (2011): 84–85.

Cui Jing. "The Study on the Holistic Governance of the Cross-Jurisdiction Public Affairs: A Case Study of the Beijing-Tianjin-Hebei Metropolitan in China". *Journal of Political Science*, vol. 2 (2012): 92.

Cui Lu, Wang Shuming. "Study on the Low Efficiency Trans-boundary Watershed Environmental Policy in China-An Example of Benefit Mechanism Analysis of Basin Management in Bohai Rim Region" in *Di san jiequanguokejizhexue ji jiaochaxuekeyanjiushengluntanwenji* [*The Third National Philosophy of Science and Technology and Interdisciplinary Graduate Forum*], (2010).

Deleon, Peter, and Danielle M. Varda. 2009. Toward a Theory of Collaborative Policy Networks: Identifying Structural Tendencies. *Policy Studies Journal* 37: 59–74.

Deneckere, Raymond and Carl Davidson. "Incentives to Form Coalitions with Bertrand Competition," RAND *Journal of Economics*, vol. 16, no. 4 (1985).

Dommel, Paul R. "Intergovernmental Relations," in Richard D. Bingham (ed.), *Management Local Government: Public Administration in Practice*. Beijing: Peking University Press, 1997: 166–177.

Dunleavy, Patrick, Helen Margetts, Simon Bastow and Jane Tinkler, *Digital Era Governance: IT Corporations, the State, and E-Government*. Oxford: Oxford University Press, 2006.

Dunleavy, Patrick, Helen Margetts, Simon Bastow and Jane Tinkler. "New Public Management Is Dead: Long Live Digital-Era Governance," *Journal of Public Administration Research and Theory*, vol. 16, no. 3 (2006).

Fan Jie (ed.). *Research on Regional Comprehensive Planning of Beijing Tianjin Hebei Metropolitan Coordinating Region*. Beijing: Beijing Science Press, 2008. p. 65.

Feiock, Richard C. 2004. *Metropolitan Governance: Conflict, Competition, and Cooperation*. Washington, D.C.: Georgetown University Press, 2004. p. 7.

Feiock Richard C. and John T. Scholz, *Self-Organizing Federalism: Collaborative Mechanisms to Mitigate Institutional Collective Action Dilemmas*. New York: Cambridge University Press, 2010: 3–6.

Feng Bangyan, Yin Laisheng. "Chengshiqunquyuzhilijiegou de dongtaiyanbian: yizhujiangsanjiaozhouweili" ["Dynamic Evolution of Urban Community Regional Governance Structure: Taking the Pearl River Delta as an example"]. *Chengshiwenti* [*Urban Problems*], vol. 7 (2011): 11–15.

Feng Xingyuan, "Lunxiaquzhengfujian de zhidujingzheng" ["Study on Inter-jurisdictional Institutional Competition"]. *Guojiaxingzhengyueyuanxuebao* [*Journal of Chinese Academy of Governance*], vol. 6 (2001).

Feng Xingyuan. "Lunxiaquzhengfujian de zhidujingzheng" ["System Competition among Jurisdictional Governments"]. *Guojiaxingzhengxueyuanxuebao* [*Journal of National School of Administration*], vol. 6 (2001): 27–32.

Ferris, James and Elizabeth Graddy. "Contracting Out: For What? With Whom?" *Public Administration Review*, vol. 46, no. 4 (1986).

Fu Yongchao, Xu Xiaolin. "Fuji guanlililun yu changzhutanchengshiqun zhengfuhezuojizhi" ["Intergovernmental Management Theory and Changsha-Zhuzhou-Xiangtan Governments Cooperation Mechanism"]. *Gonggongguanlixuebao* [*Journal of Public Management*], vol. 4, no. 2 (April 2007): 24–29.

Gao Jianhua. "Quyugonggongguanlishiyuxia de zhengtixingzhili: kuajiezhili de yigefenxikuangjia" ["The Holistic Governance of Governments' Cooperation under the Regional Public Management Perspective: An Analysis Framework of Cross-border Governance"]. *Zhongguoxingzhengguanli* [*Chinese Public Administration*], vol. 11 (2010): 77–81.

Goldsmith, Stephen and William D. Eggers, *Governing by Network: The New Shape of the Public Sector.* Washington, D. C.: Brookings Institution Press, 2004.

Gray, Barbara and Donna Wood. "Collaborative Alliances: Moving from Practice to Theory," *Journal of Applied Behavioral Science*, vol. 27, no. 1 (1991).

Guo Jiulin, "A Comprehensive Survey of the American Metropolitan Belt and its Implications," *Economic Geography*, vol. 2 (2008).

Hardin, Russell. *Collective Action.* Baltimore, MD: Johns Hopkins University Press, 1982.

Hu Xuwei, Zhou Yixing, et al., *Study on Spatial Agglomeration and Diffusion of China's Coastal Cities and Towns.* Beijing: Science Press, 2000.

Hu Yi, Chen Ruilian. "Fadaguojia de liuyushuiwurangonggongzhilijizhijiqiqishi" ["Public Governance Mechanism of River Basin Pollution in Developed Country and Its Enlightenment"]. *Tianjin xingzhengxueyuanxuebao* [*Journal of Tianjin Administration Institute*], vol. 1 (2006).

Hu Yi, Chen Ruilian. "Fadaguojia de liuyushuiwurangonggongzhilijizhijiqiqishi" ["Enlightenment of governance mechanism of water pollution for drainage basin in developed countries"]. *Tianjin xingzhengxingyuanxuebao* [*Journal of Tianjin Administration Institute*] vol. 8, no. 1 (February 2006): 37–40.

Hu Yi, Li Yuansheng. "Lunliuyuqujishengtaibaohubuchangjizhi de goujian—yiminjiangliuyuweili" ["The Establishment of the Inter-catchment's Ecological Compensation System"]. *Fujianshifandaxuexuebao (zhexueshehuikexue ban)* [*Journal of Fujian Normal University (Philosophy and Social Sciences Edition)*], no. 6 (2006): 53–58.

Hu Yi. "Huanjingbaohu Zhong zhengfuyuqiyehuobanzhilijizhi" ["Government and corporate partner governance mechanism in environmental protection"]. *Xingzhengluntan* [*Administrative Tribune*], vol. 4 (2008): 80–82.

Hunan Public Management Research Base. "Changzhutanshiyanquguanlijigoushezhiyanjiu" ["Research on Establishment of Management Institutions in Chang-Zhu-Tan Pilot-area"]. *Zhongguoxingzhengguanli* [*Chinese Public Administration*] vol. 2 (2010): 85–88.

Jacobs, Jane. *The Death and Life of Great American Cities*, New York: Random House, 1961: 447.

Jin, Taijun, and Yuqing Tang. 2011. "The Dilemma of the Collaborative Governance of Regional Ecology and its Solutions". *Journal of Nanjing Normal University (Social Science Edition)*, vol. 5: 17–21.

Jin Taijun. "Cong xingzhengquxingzhengdaoquyugonggongguanli—zhengfuzhilixingtaishanbian de boyifenxi" ["From administering administrative divisions to regional public administration: A game analysis of evolution in the pattern of governance by the government"]. *Zhongguoshehuikexue* [*Social Sciences in China*] vol. XXIX, no. 4 (November 2008): 48–62.

Jin Taijun. "From Administrative Region Administration to Regional Public Management: A Game Analysis of the Evolution of Government Governance." *The Chinese Social Sciences*, vol. 6 (2007).

de Leon, Peter and Danielle Varda. "Toward a Theory of Collaborative Policy Networks: Identifying Structural Tendencies," *The Policy Studies Journal*, vol. 37, no. 1 (2009).

LeRoux, Kelly, Paul W. Brandenburger and Sanjay K. Pandey. "Interlocal Service Cooperation in U.S. Cities: A Social Network Explanation," *Public Administration Review*, vol. 70, no. 2 (2010).

Li Ruichang. "Gonggongzhilizhuanxing: zhengtizhuyifuxing" ["Transformation of Public Governance: Holism's Renaissance"]. *Jiangsu xingzhengxueyuanxuebao* [*Journal of Jiangsu Administration institute*], vol. 46, no. 4 (2009): 102–107.

Li Ying, Jiang Guzheng. "Liuyushuiziyuankaifaguihua Zhong zhanluehuanping de zuoyong—yichangjiangkouzonghezhengzhiguihuahuanpingweili" ["The role of strategic environmental assessment in river basin water resources development planning: a case study of comprehensive environment assessment of the Yangtze River estuary"]. *Renmin Changjiang* [*Yangtze River*], vol. 8 (2010): 40–42.

Li Yuansheng, Hu Yi. "Cong kecengdaowangluo: liuyuzhilijizhichuangxin de lujingxuanze" ["From the bureaucracy to the network: Path Choice of Innovation in River Basin Governance Mechanism"]. *Fuzhou dangxiaoxuebao* [*Journal of the Party School of Fuzhou*], vol. 2 (2010): 35–39.

Lin Shangli, *Guoneizhengfujianguanxi* [*Domestic intergovernmental relations*]. Hangzhou: Zhejiang renminchubanshe [Hangzhou: Zhejiang People's Publishing House], 1998.

Lin Ka, Li Yong, Shen Qiu. "Shehuiguanlichuangxin he tuijinduoyuanzhutifazhan de hangzhoujingyanyanjiu" ["Study on the Hangzhou Experience of Social Management Innovation and the Promotion of Multiple Social Subjects' Development"]. *Shehuikexuezhanxian* [*Social Science Frontier*], vol. 3 (2013).

Lipecap, Gary. *Contracting for Property Rights.* New York: Cambridge University Press, 1989.

Liu Bo, Wang Lili, Yao yinliang. "Zhengtixingzhiliyuwangluozhili de bijiaoyanjiu" ["A Comparative Study of Holistic Governance and Network Governance"]. *Jingjishehuitizhibijiao* [*Comparative Economic & Social Systems*], vol. 5 (2011): 134–140.

Liu Guihuan, Zhang Huiyuan, Wang Jinnan. "Huan jingjinpinkundai de shengtaibuchangjizhitansuo" ["Study on the Ecological Compensation Mechanism in the Poverty Belt around Beijing and Tianjin"] in *Zhongguohuanjingkexuexuehuixueshunianhuiyouxiulunwenji* [*Proceedings of the Academic Annual Conference of Chinese Environmental Sciences Association, 2006*], (2006).

Liu Junde. "Lun zhonguo dalu dadushiqu xingzhengzuzhi yu guanlimoshi chuangxin-jianlun zhujiangsanjiaozhou de zhengqugaige" ["Study on the innovation of the administrative organization and management of the metropolitan areas in Chinese mainland: A case study on the administrative innovation of the pearl river delta"]. *Jingjidili* [*Economic Geography*], vol. 21, no. 2 (March 2001): 201–207.

Liu Junde, "An Analysis of the Phenomenon of 'Administrative Region Economy' Highlighted in the Transition Period of China," *Theoretical Front*, vol. 10 (2004).

Liu Yaping, Liu Linlin. "Zhongguoquyuzhengfuhezuo de kunjingyuzhanwang" ["Predicament and Prospect of the Cooperation among China's Local Governments"]. *Xueshuyanjiu* [*Academic Research*], vol. 12 (2012): 38–45.

Liu Yaping, *Dangdaizhongguodifangzhengfujianjingzheng* [*Competition among local governments in contemporary China*]. Beijing: Shehuikexuewenxianchubanshe [Beijing: Social Science Literature Publishing House], 2007.

Logan, John R. and Harvey L. Molotch, *Urban Fortunes: The Political Economy of Place*. Berkeley: University of California Press, 1987: 53–65.

Logsdon, Jeanne M. "Interests and Interdependence in the Formation of Problem-Solving Collaborations," *Journal of Applied Behavioral Science*, vol. 27, no. 1 (1991).

Lubell, Mark, Mark Schneider, John Scholz and Mihriye Mete. "Watershed Partnerships and the Emergence of Collective Action Institutions," *American Journal of Political Science*, vol. 46, no. 1 (2002).

Lu Da, Pan Haitao. "Huan jingjinpinkundaifachujingshizhiyan" ["The poverty Belt around Beijing and Tianjin Gives Warning Words"]. *Zhongguogaige bao* [*China Reform News*] (September 19, 2005).

Luo Chuanling. "xinxihuayuchangzhutanchengshiqun 'Liangxingshehui' jianshechutan" ["Research on information-based system and the resource-saving and environment-friendly in the Chang-Zhu-Tan city group"]. *Jingjidili* [*Economic Geography*], vol. 29, no. 3 (March 2009): 415–419.

Luo Haiming, Tang Jin, Hu Lingqian and Wang Jie: "New Progress in Defining Index Systems in Metropolitan Areas of the United States," *Foreign Urban Planning*, vol. 3 (2005).

Ma Hailong: "History, Present Situation and Future: on Regional Cooperation in Beijing, Tianjin and Hebei Province," *Economist*, vol. 5, (2009).

Molotch, Harvey L. "The City as a Growth Machine," *The American Journal of Sociology*, vol. 82, no. 2 (1976).

Mu Aiying, Wu Jianqi, Wu Yiqing, *Jingjinji: Linian, moshiyujizhi* [*Beijing-Tianjin-Hebei: Ideas, Models and Mechanisms*]. Beijing: Zhongguoshehuikexuechubanshe [*Beijing: Chinese Social Science Press*], 2010.

Oakerson, Ronald J. *Governing Local Public Economics: Creating the Civic Metropolis*. Oakland, CA: ICS Press, 1999.

Oakerson, Ronald J. "The Study of Metropolitan Governance," in *Metropolitan Governance: Conflict, Competition, and Cooperation*, edited by Richard C. Feiock, Washington, D.C.: Georgetown University Press, 2004.

Olson, Mancur. *The Logic of Collective Action*. Cambridge, MA: Harvard University Press, 1971.

Osborne, David and Ted Gaebler, *Reinventing Government: How the Entrepreneurial Spirit Is Transforming the Public Sector*, Reading, MA: Addison-Wesley, 1992.

Ostrom, Elinor. *Governing the Commons.* New York: Cambridge University Press, 1990.

Ostrom, Elinor, Roy Gardner and James Walker, *Rules, Games, and Common-Pool Resources.* Ann Arbor: University of Michigan Press, 1994.

Ostrom, Vincent and Charles Tiebout and Robert Warren. "The Organization of Governance in Metropolitan Areas: A Theoretical Inquiry," *American Political Science Review*, vol. 55 (1961).

Ostrom, Vincent, Robert, L. Bish and Elinor, Ostrom, *Local Government in the United States*, San Francisco, ICS Press, 72–80.

O'Toole, Laurence J., Jr. "Treating Networks Seriously: Practical and Research-Based Agendas in Public Administration." *Public Administration Review*, vol. 57, no. 1 (1997): 45–52

Peng Jinpeng. "Quanguanxingzhili: Lilunyuzhiduhuacelue" ["Holistic Governance: Theory and Institutionalization Strategies"].] *Zhengzhikexueluncong (Taiwan)* [*Political Science Review (Taiwan)*], vol. 23 (2005).

Perri 6, Diana Leat, Kimberly Seltzer and Gerry Stoker, *Towards Holistic Governance: The New Reform Agenda.* New York: Palgrave, 2002.

Perri 6, *Governing in the Round: Strategies for Holistic Government*, London: Demos, 1999.

Pollitt, Christopher. "Joined-up Government: A Survey," *Political Studies Review*, vol. 1, no. 1 (2003).

Post, Stephanie S. "Metropolitan Area Governance and Institutional Collective Action," in *Metropolitan Governance: Conflict, Competition, and Cooperation*, edited by Richard C. Feiock, Washington, D.C.: Georgetown University Press, 2004: 67–92.

Radin, Beryl A., Robert Agranoff, Ann O' M Bowman, et al., *New Governance for Rural America: Creating Intergovernmental Partnerships.* Lawrence: University Press of Kansas, 1996.

Ran Ran. "Yalixingtizhixia de zhengzhijiliyudifangzhengfuhuanjingzhili" ["Political Incentives and Local Environmental Governance Under a 'Pressurized System'"]. *Jingjishehuitizhibijiao* [*Comparative Economic & Social Systems*], vol. 3 (2013).

Research Group, Poverty Belt around Beijing and Tianjin Issue. "Dui huanjingjin-pinkundaifazhanxianzhuangyuduice de genzongyanjiu" ["Tracking Research on the Development Status and Countermeasures of the Poverty Belt around Beijing and Tianjin"] in Qi Benchao, Jing Tihua (ed.). *2009–2010 zhongguoquyujingjifazhanbaogao* [*2009–2010 Annual Report on China's Regional Economy*]. Beijing, Shehuikexuewenxianchubanshe [Beijing: Social Sciences Academic Press], 2010: 176–177.

Research Group, Regional Cooperation in the Poverty Belt around Beijing and Tianjin. "Xiaochuhuanjingjinpinkundan, cujinjingjinyiquyuxietiaofazhan" ["Removal of the Poverty Belt around Beijing and Tianjin, Promotion of the Coordinated Development of the Beijing-Tianjin-Hebei Region"] in Jing Tihua (ed.). *2004–2005 zhongguoquyujingjifazhanbaogao* [*2004–2005 Annual Report on China's Regional Economy*]. Beijing, Shehuikexuewenxianchubanshe [Beijing: Social Sciences Academic Press], 2010, p. 177.

Riker, Willian and Itai Sened. "A Political Theory of the Origin of Property Rights: Airport Slots," *American Journal of Political Science*, vol. 35, no. 4 (1991).

Savitch, H. V. and R. K. Vogel, *Regional Politics: American in A Post-city Age*. Thousand Oaks, CA: Sage Publications, 1996: 110, 112.

Savitch, H. V. and R. K. Vogel. "Paths to New Regionalism," *State and Local Government Review*, vol. 32, no. 3 (2000): 158–168.

Savitch, H. V., R. Vogel, Ye Lin. "Beyond the Rhetoric: Lessons from Louisville's Consolidation," *American Review of Public Administration*, vol. 40, no. 1 (2010).

Savitch, H. V. "Territory and Power: Rescaling for a Global Era," *Proceedings of the International Conference on Urban and Regional Development in the 21st Century*, Sun Yat-sen University, December 17–18, 2011.

Shen Chengcheng, JinTaijun. "'Tuoyu' gonggongweijizhili yu quyugonggong-guanlitizhichuangxin" ["'Disembodying' Public Crisis Management and Innovation of Regional Public Administration System"]. *Jianghaixuekan* [*Jiang-hai Academic Journal*] no. 1 (2011): 107–112+238.

Shi Jianya. *The City of Late Chinese Empire*, Beijing, China Publishing House, 2000: 2–3.

Shu Qing, Zhou Keyu. *From Closure to Openness: Perspective of Chinese Administrative Economy*, Shanghai, East China Normal University Press, 2003.

Shu Qing, Zhou Keyu, *Cong fengbizouxiangkaifang: zhongguoxingzhengqujingji-toushi* [*From Closed to Open: Perspective of the "Administrative Regional Economy" in China*]. Shanghai: Huadongshifandaxuechubanshe [Shanghai: East China Normal University Press], 2004 and Liu Junde. "Zhongguozhuanxing-qituxian de xingzhengqujingjixianxiangfenxi" [Analysis on the Prominent "Administrative Regional Economy" Phenomenon in China's Transitional Period]. Lilunqianyan [Theory Front], vol. 10 (2004).

Shu, Qing, and Keyu Zhou. *From Closed to Open: The Analysis of Administrative Area Economy in China*. Shanghai: East China Normal University Press, 2003.

Sivan Vgen and Chris Huxham. "Nurturing Collaborative Relations: Building Trust in Interorganizational Collaboration," *Journal of Applied Behavioral Science*, vol. 39, no. 1 (2003).

Stein, Robert. *Urban Alternatives: Public and Private Markets in the Provision of Local Services*. Pittsburgh, PA: University of Pittsburgh Press, 1990.

Steinacker, Annette. "Game-Theoretic Models of Metropolitan Cooperation," in Richard C. Feiock (ed.), *Metropolitan Governance: Conflict, Competition, and Cooperation*. Washington, D.C.: Georgetown University Press, 2004: 47–51.

Post, Stephanie S. "Metropolitan Area Governance and Institutional Collective Action," in Richard C. Feiock (ed.), *Metropolitan Governance: Conflict, Competition, and Cooperation*. Washington, D.C.: Georgetown University Press, 2004: 70–79.

Tao Xidong: "Study on the Economic Analysis and Integration Mechanism of the Administrative Region of Trans-provincial Metropolitan Area: Take Xuzhou Metropolitan Area as an Example," *Doctoral Dissertation of East China Normal University*, 2004.

Tao Xidong: "Trans Regional Governance: A New Approach to Economic Integration in China's Trans Provincial Metropolitan Coordinating Region," *Geographical Science*, vol. 5 (2005).

Thaler, Richard H. "Anomalies: The Ultimatum Game," *Journal of Economic Perspectives*, vol 2, no. 4 (1998): 95–206.

Wallis, Allan D. "Inventing Regionalism: A Two-phase Approach," *National Civic Review*, vol. 83, no. 3 (Fall–Winter 1994).

Wallis, Allan D. "The Third Wave: Current Trends in Regional Governance," *National Civic Review*, vol. 83, no. 3 (Summer–Fall 1994): 290–310.

Wang Dianli. "Bandaochengshiqunfazhan dongle yuzhangai de xingzhengxuefenxi" ["Administrative Analysis of the Driving Forces and Obstacles of Peninsula City Group Development"]. *Dongyueluncong [Dongyue Tribune]*, vol. 30, no. 5 (May 2009): 30–34.

Wang Dianli. "Quyugonggongguanli de zhiduyujizhichuangxintanxi: yi Shandong bandaochengshiqunweili" ["Analysis on the Innovation of System and Mechanism of Regional Public Management: Taking Shandong Peninsula Urban Agglomeration as an Example"]. *Beijing xingzhengxueyuanxuebao [Journal of Beijing Administrative College]*, vol. 5 (2009): 11–15.

Wang Fengyun, *Hexiegongjinzhong de zhengfuxietiao: changsanjiaochengshiqun de shizhengyanjiu [Government Coordination in Harmony and Progress: An Empirical Study of the Yangtze River Delta Urban Agglomeration]*. Guangzhou: Zhongshandaxuechubanshe [Guangzhou: Sun Yat-sen University Press], 2009.

Wang Jian, Bao Jing, Liu Xiaokang, Wang Dianli. " 'Fuhexingzheng' de tichu— jiejuedangdaizhongguoquyujingjiyitihuayuxingzhengquhuachongtu de xinsilu" ["Proposal of 'combined administration': A New Way to Solve the Conflicts between Regional Economic Integration and Administrative Divisions in Contemporary China"]. *Zhongguoxingzhengguanli* [Chinese Public Administration] vol. 3 (2004): 44–48.

Wang, Jian, Bao Jing, Liu Xiaokang, Wang Dianli: "The Proposition of 'Compound Administration'—A New Idea to Solve the Conflict between Regional Economic Integration and Administrative Division in Contemporary China," *Administrative Administration of China*, vol. 3 (2004).

Wang, Junfeng. "Zhongguoliuyushengtaibuchangjizhi shishikuangjia yu buchangmoshiyanjiu: jiyu buchangzijinlaiyuan de shijiao" ["Research on Implementation Framework of Ecological Compensation Mechanism and Compensation Mode: From the Prospect of Compensation Funds Source"]. *Zhongguorenkouziyuanyuhuanjing [China Population, Resources and Environment]*, vol. 2 (2013).

Wang Xu, Luo Sidong. *Local Government in the New Urbanization Period of the United States: The Game Between Regional Coordination and Local Autonomy*. Xiamen University Press, 2010. p. 43–45+295.

Wasserman, Stanley, and Katherine Faust. *Social Network Analysis: Methods and Application*. Cambridge University Press. 1994.

Waste, R. W. *The Ecology of City Policymaking*. New York: Oxford University Press, 1989.

Wei Hongxia. "Huan jingjinpinkundai yu jingjinshengtaianquan" ["Poverty Belt around Beijing and Tianjin" and "Ecological Security in Beijing and Tianjin"]. *Hebei linye* [*Hebei Forestry*], vol. 5 (2006).

Wei Wei and Zhao Guangrui: "A Review of the Patterns of Metropolitan Coordinating Region in Japan," *Modern Japanese Economy*, vol. 2 (2005).

Williamson, Oliver. *Market and Hierarchies*. New York: Free Press, 1975.

Wu, Aiming, Cui Jing, Qi Guanghua. "Yunyongdianzizhengwu tuijin shixianzhengfu jizhongbangong" ["Promoting the Centralized Work in Municipal and County Governments through E-government"]. *Zhongguoxingzhengguanli* [*Chinese Public Administration*], vol. 5 (2011): 34–37.

Xie, Qinkui. "Zhongguozhengfu de fujiguanxiyanjiu" ["Intergovernmental Relations in China"]. *Beijing daxuexuebao (zhexueshehuikexue ban)* [*Journal of Peking University (Humanities and Social Science)*], vol. 37, no. 197 (2000): 26–34.

Xie, Shouhong, Ning Yuemin. "Dushuqu: Changzhutanyitihua de biyouzhilu" ["Metropolitan area: The only way of integration for Chang-Zhu-Tan area"]. *Jingjidili* [*Economic Geography*] vol. 25, no. 6 (November 2005): 834–837.

Xie, Shouhong. "Conceptual Definition and Comparative Analysis of Metropolitan Area, Metropolitan Coordinating Region and Metropolitan Belt," *Urban Issues*, vol. 6 (2008).

Xing, Hua. "Shuiziyuanguanlixiezuojizhiguancha: Liuyuyuxingzhengquyufengong" ["The Observation of the Cooperation Mechanism of Water Resources Management: The river basin and the Administrative Regional Division"]. *Gaige* [*Reform*], vol. 5 (2011): 68–73.

Xinhuawang. "Changsanjiao chengshijingji xietiao huicheng guonei shouge duli bangong quyu hezuo zuzhi" ["Yangtze River Delta Urban Economic Coordination Association became the first independent office cooperation organization in China"], http://news.xinhuanet.com/fortune/2012-04/18/c_111803470.htm, accessed on April 18, 2012.

Yang, Aiping, Chen Ruilian. "Cong Xingzhengquxingzhengdaoquyugonggonggua nli-zhengfuzhilixingtaishanbian de yizhongbijiaofenxi" ["From 'Administrative District Administration' to 'Regional Public Management': A Comparative Analysis of the Evolution of Government Governance"]. *Jiangxishehuikexue* [*Jiangxi Social Sciences*], vol. 11 (2004): 23–31.

Yang, Aiping. "Cong chuizhijilidaopingxingjili: difangzhengfuhezuo de liyijilijizhichuangxin" ["From Vertical Incentive to Horizontal Incentive: as an Innovation of Benefit Encouragement Mechanism in Local Government Cooperation"]. *Xueshuyanjiu* [*Academic Research*], vol. 5 (2011): 47–53.

Yang, Aiping. "Cong zhengzhidongyuandaozhidujianshe: zhusanjiaoyitihuazhong de zhengfuchuangxin" ["From Political Mobilization to Institutional Construction: Government Innovation in Pearl River Delta's Integration"]. *Huanan shifandaxuexuebao (shehuikexue ban)* [*Journal of South China Normal University (Social Science Edition)*], vol. 6 (2011): 114–120.

Yang, Aiping. "Lun quyuyitihuaxia de quyuzhengfujian hezuo: dongyin, moshi jizhanwang" ["On Interregional Government Cooperation under Regional

Integration—Motivation, model and outlook"]. *Zhengzhixueyanjiu* [*Cass Journal of Political Science*], vol. 3 (2007): 77–86.

Yang, Aiping. "Quyuhezuozhong de fujiqiyue: gainianyufenlei" ["A Research on Intergovernmental Agreement for Regional Cooperation: Concept and Classification"]. *Zhongguoxingzhengguanli* [*Chinese Public Administration*], vol. 6 (2011): 100–104.

Yang, Aiping. 2011. "From Vertical Incentives to Horizontal Incentives: The Innovation of Interest Motivation Mechanism of Local Government Collaboration". *Academic Research,* vol. 5 (2011): 47–53.

Yang, Lianyun, Shi Yabi. "Jingjinyiquyuxietiaofazhan de zhanluesikao" ["The Strategic Thinking of Harmonious Development of Beijing, Tianjin, and Hebei"]. *Hebei xueken* [*Hebei Academic Journal*], vol. 4 (2006).

Yang, Lianyun, Li Hongmin. "Huan jingjinpinkundai de xianzhuangyufazhanzhanlueyanjiu" ["Research on the Present Situation and Development Strategy of the Poverty Belt around Beijing and Tianjin"] in Jing Tihua (ed.). *2005–2006 zhongguo quyujingji fazhanbaogao* [*2005–2006 Annual Report on China's Regional Economy*]. Beijing, Shehuikexuewenxianchubanshe [Beijing: Social Sciences Academic Press], 2006: 94–95.

Yang, Long and Peng Yanqiang. "Lijiezhongguo defang zhengfuhezuo—xingzhengguanxiaquanrangdu de shijiao" ["Understanding the Cooperation of Local Government in China—from the Perspective of Administrative Jurisdiction Transfer"]. *Zhengzhixueyanjiu* [*Cass Journal of Political Science*], vol. 4 (2009): 61–66.

Yang, Long, Zheng Chunyong. "Difanghezuo dui zhengfujianguanxi de tuozhan" ["Local cooperation to expand intergovernmental relations"]. *Tansuoyuzhengming* [*Exploration and Free Views*], vol. 1 (2011): 38–41.

Yang, Yan and Sun Tao. "Kuaquyuhuanjingzhiliyudifangzhengfuhezuojizhiyanjiu" ["Study on the Mechanism of Local Government Cooperation in Interregional Environment Governance"]. *Zhongguoxingzhengguanli* [*Chinese Public Administration*], vol. 1 (2009): 66–69.

Yang, Zhengbo. "Laiyinhebaohu de guojihezuojizhi" ["International cooperation mechanism for the protection of the Rhine"]. *Shuilishuidiankuaibao* [*Express Water Resources & Hydropower Information*], vol. 1 (2008): 5–7.

Yang, Long, and Yanqiang Peng. "The Study on the Local Government Cooperation in China from the Perspective of the Assignment of Administrative Jurisdiction". *Journal of Political Science*, vol. 4 (2009): 61–64.

Yao Xianguo, Xie Xiaobo: "The Analysis of the Competition Behavior of Local Government in the Economic Integration of Yangtze River Delta". *Journal of the Party School of the CPC Zhejiang Provincial Committee*, vol. 3 (2004).

Yao, Yinliang, Liu Bo, Wang Yingluo. "Difangzhengfuwangluozhiliyuhexieshehuigoujian de liluntantao" ["The Network Governance of Local Government and The Construction of Harmonious Society"]. *Zhongguoxingzhengguanli* [*Chinese Public Administration*], vol. 11 (2009): 91–94.

Yao, Yinliang, Liu Bo, Wang Yingluo. "Wangluozhilililunzaidifangzhengfugonggongguanlishijianzhong de yunyongjiqi dui xingzhengtizhigaige de qishi" ["The Application of theory of network governance in the practice of local government public management and Its Enlightenment to the Reform of Administrative System"]. *Renwenzazhi* [*The Journal of Humanities*], vol. 1 (2010): 76–85.

Ye, Lin. "Xin quyuzhuyi de xingqiyufazhan: yigezongshu" ["A Review of Literature on New Regionalism"]. *Gonggongxingzhengpinglun* [*Journal of Public Administration*], vol. 3 (2010): 175–190.

Ye, Lin. "Zhaohuizhengfu: hougonggongguanlishiyuxia de quyuzhilitansuo" ["Retrieving the Government: Exploring Regional Governance from the Perspective of Post-New Public Management"]. *Xueshuyanjiu* [*Academic Research*], vol. 5 (2012): 64–69.

Ye, Lin. "Regional Government and Governance in China and the United States". *Public Administration Review*, 2009, s116–121.

Yin, Yifen. "Wangluozhili: Gonggongguanli de xinkuangjia" ["Network Governance: A New Framework of Public Administration"]. *Gonggongguanlixuebao* [*Journal of Public Management*], vol. 4, no. 1 (January 2007): 89–96+126.

Yu, Gangqiang, CaiLihui. "Zhongguodushiqunwangluohuazhilimoshiyanjiu" ["Governance by Network: The New Trend of Governing Pattern of Urban Agglomeration in China"]. *Zhongguoxingzhengguanli* [*Chinese Public Administration*], vol. 6 (2011): 93–98.

Yu, Minjiang. "Lunshengtaizhilizhong de zhongyangyudifangzhengfujianliyixietiao" ["Interests Coordination Between Central and Local Governments on Ecological Governance"]. *Shehuikexue* [*Social Sciences*], vol. 9 (2011).

Yu, Gangqiang, and Lihui Cai. "The Study on the Network Governance Patterns of the Metropolitan in China". *Chinese Public Administration*, vol. 6 (2011): 96.

Zhai Lei. "Difangzhengfuxietongzhili de xianzhuangyuqushi" ["The status quo and trend of local government collaborative governance"], in Zhu Guanglei (ed.), *Chinese Government Development Research Report (3rd Series): Local Government Development and Intergovernmental Relations*. Beijing: Zhongguorenmindaxuechubanshe [China Renmin University Press], 2013: 140.

Zhang Jingen, "Fujizhili: dangdaizhongguofujiguanxiyanjiu de xinquxiang" ["Intergovernmental Governance: The New Trend for Research on Intergovernmental Relations in Current China"]. *Xueshuyanjiu* [*Academic Research*], vol. 2 (2013).

Zhang, Jingen. "Cong quyuxingzhengdaoquyuzhili: dangdaizhongguoquyujingjiyitihua de fazhanluxiang" ["On the Development Rout of Current China's Regional Economy Unity: from Regional Administration to a Region Governed"]. *Xueshuyanjiu* [*Academic Research*], vol. 9 (2009): 42–49.

Zhang, Jingen. "Quyugonggongguanlizhiduchuangxinfenxi" ["Analysis of regional public management system innovation: Taking the Pearl River Delta as an example"]. *Zhengzhixueyanjiu* [*Cass Journal of Political Science*], vol. 3 (2010): 63–75.

Zhang, Jingen. "Shilunxinquyuzhuyishiyexia de fan zhusanjiaoquyuhezuo" ["On Regional Cooperation from View of New Regionalism in the Pan-Pearl River Delta"]. *Wuhan daxuexuebao* [*Wuhan University Journal (Philosophy & Social Sciences)*], vol. 61, no. 3 (May 2008): 351–357.

Zhang, Jingen. "Xin quyuzhuyi: meiguodadushiquzhili de xinsilu" ["New Regionalism: New Ideas for the Management of American Metropolitan Areas"].

*Zhongshandaxuexuebao* [*Journal of Sun Yat-sen university (social science edition)*], vol. 50, no. 1 (2010): 131–141.

Zhang, Jingxiang, Zou Jun, et al. "A Study on the Organization of Regional Space in Metropolitan Coordinating Region," *Urban Planning*, vol, 5 (2001).

Zhang, Keyun. *Quyudazhanyuquyujingji de guanxi* [*Regional war and regional economic relations*]. Beijing: Minzhuyujianshechubanshe [Beijing: Democracy and Construction Press], 2001.

Zhang, Tingwei. "Urban Development and a Socialist Pro-growth Coalition in Shanghai," *Urban Affairs Review,* vol. 37, No. 4, (2002).

Zhang, Wei. "Concept, Characteristics and Planning of Metropolitan Coordinating Region," *Urban Planning*, vol. 6 (2003).

Zhang, Zhaishu. "Chengshiyitiyushehuifuhezhuti de lianhezhili: dui hangzhou 3 zhongchengshizhilishijian de zuzhifenxi" ["Urban Issues and Social Multiple Agents' Joint Governance"]. *Guanlishijie* [*Management World*], vol. 2 (2012).

Zhang, Zhenhua. "Zengzhanglianmeng: fenxi zhuanxingqi woguodifangzhengfu yu jingjiliyijituanguanxi de yizhonglilunshijiao" ["Growth Coalition: A Theoretical Perspective to Analyze the Relation Between Local Government and Economic Interest Group In China's Transitional Period"]. *Tianjin shehuikexue* [*Tianjin Social Sciences*], vol. 1 (2011).

Zhang, Xu, and Xiaorui Zhang. "The Win-Win Integration of the Capital Economic Circle Driving on the Fast Track". *Beijing News*: B04. 2011.

Zhao Feng, Jiang Debo. "Changsanjiaoquyuhezuojizhi de jingyanyujinyibufazhansilu" ["Experience and Further Developing Route of the Cooperative Mechanism for Yangtze River Delta"]. *Zhongguoxingzhengguanli* [*Chinese Public Administration*], vol. 2 (2011): 81–84.

Zhao, Huaying. "Huanjingjinjipinkundai zhilizhong de difangzhengfu hengxiangfujihezuojizhi goujian yanjiu" ["Study on the Construction of Horizontal Inter-Government Cooperation Mechanism of Local Governments in the Governance of the Beijing-Tianjin Poverty Belt"]. *Shanghaishifandaxueshuoshilunwen* [*Master thesis of Shanghai Normal University*], 2012.

Zhao, Yu, "Dui huanjingjinpinkundai de fuchibuchangjizhiyanjiu" ["Research on the Support and Compensation Mechanism of the Poverty Belt around Beijing and Tianjin"]. *Jingjiwentiyanjiu* [*Inquiry into Economic Issues*], vol. 3 (2008).

Zhou, Li-an. "Jinshengboyizhong zhengfuguanyuan de jiliyuhezuo: jianlun woguodifangbaohuzhuyi he chongfujianshewenti changqicunzai de yuanyin" ["The Incentive and Cooperation of Government Officials in the Political Tournaments: An Interpretation of the Prolonged Local Protection and Duplicative Investments in China"]. *Jingjiyanjiu* [*Economic Research Journal*], vol. 6 (2004).

Zhou, Li-an. "Zhongguodifangguanyuan de jinshengjinbiaosaimoshiyanjiu" ["Governing China's Local Officials: An Analysis of Promotion Tournament Model"]. *Jingjiyanjiu* [*Economic Research Journal*], vol. 7 (2007): 36–50.

Zhou, Li-an, *Zhuanxingzhong de difangzhengfu: guanyuanjiliyuzhili* [*Local Government in Transition: Officials' Incentive and Governance*]. Shanghai: Shanghai renminchubanshe [Shanghai People's Publishing House], 2008, 252–257.

Zhou, Li-an. "Guanyuanjinshengjingzhengyubianjiexiaoying: yishengqujiaojiedidai de jingjifazhanweili" ["Official promotion competition and border effect:

Taking the economic development of the provincial border area as an example"]. *Jinrongyanjiu* [*Journal of Financial Research*], vol. 3 (2011): 15–26.

Zhou, Li-an. "Jinshengboyi Zhong zhengfuguanyuan de jiliyuhezuo—jianlun-woguo defang baohuzhuyi he chongfujianshewentichangqicunzai de yuanyin" ["The Incentive and Cooperation of Government Officials in the Political Tour-naments: An Interpretation of the Prolonged Local Protectionism and Duplica-tive Investments in China"]. *Jingjiyanjiu* [*Economic Research Journal*], vol. 6 (2004): 33–40.

Zhou, Lian. "The Encouragement and Cooperation of Government Officials in Pro-motion Game—Also on the Long-standing Causes of Local Protectionism and Repeated Construction in China," *Economic Research*, vol. 6 (2004).

Zhou, Xueguang, Lian Hong. "Zhongguozhengfu de zhilimoshi: yigekongzhiquan-lilun" ["Modes of Governance in the Chinese Bureaucracy: A 'control right' Theory"]. *Shehuixueyanjiu* [*Sociological Studies*], vol. 5 (2012).

Zhou, Xueguang. "Jicengzhengfujian de gongmouxianxiang: yigezhengfuxingwei de zhiduluoji" ["Collusion among Local Governments: The institutional logic of a government behavior"]. *Shehuixueyanjiu* [*Sociological Studies*], vol. 3 (2008).

Zhou, Zhiren, Jiang Minjuan. "Zhengtizhengfuxia de zhengcexietong: Lilun-yufadaguojia de dangdaishijian" ["Policy coordination under the overall government: Theory and contemporary practice in developed countries"]. *Guojiaxingzhengxueyuanxuebao* [*Journal of Chinese Academy of Governance*], vol. 6 (2010): 28–33.

Zhu, Erjuan. *"Shierwu" shiqijingjinjifazhanyanjiu (2009)* [*Beijing-Tianjin-Hebei Development Study during the Twelfth Five-Year Plan Period (2009)*]. Beijing: Zhongguojingjichubanshe [Beijing: China Economic Publishing House], 2010.

Zhu, Qianwei. "Cong xingonggongguanlidaozhengtixingzhili" ["From New Public Management to Holistic Governance"]. *Zhongguoxingzhengguanli* [*Chinese Public Administration*], vol. 10 (2008): 52–58.

Zou, Weixing, Zhou Liqun. "QuyujingjiyitihuaJinchengpouxi: changsanjiao, zhusanjiaoyuhuanbohai" ["Analysis of Regional Economic Integration: Yangtze River Delta, Pearl River Delta and Bohai Rim Region"]. *Gaige* [*Reform*], vol. 10 (2010): 86–93.

# Index

Silk and Women's Wear Industry
　Alliance 120
Skinner, William 3
SNA *see* social network analysis
social development 6, 35, 91, 95, 104,
　118
social management systems 98
social network analysis 13–16, 19, 91,
　95–6, 104, 110–11
social subjects 44–5, 47, 120
society 6, 16, 35–6, 45, 47, 109, 120;
　*see also* civil society
solid waste 26, 74
special funds 58, 62, 64–5, 84, 105,
　111, 113, 118; of cross-border public
　affairs in the metropolitan area 19,
　58; from cross-regional collaborative
　organizations 58; jointly funded by
　local governments 60; regional 59,
　117
spillover effects 69, 75–6, 84
stakeholders 33, 39–40, 73; economic
　33; multiple 33; social 33;
　structurally equivalent 40
strategic planning 9, 13, 15
subgroup structure of the Beijing-
　Tianjin-Hebei metropolitan
　collaborative network from 2008 to
　2011 *103*
subgroups 102–4; emerging cohesive
　91; emerging condensing 111; large
　103; multicenter 104; structure of the
　Beijing-Tianjin-Hebei metropolitan
　collaborative network from 2004 to
　2007 102, *103*
subjects 10, 19, 30, 38, 55, 60–2, 64–5,
　94; administrative 7; collaborative
　62; contract 33; independent market
　interest 68; social composite 120
system 27, 30, 33, 38, 55;
　administrative subcontracting 68–9;
　ecological evaluation index 85;
　federal constitutional 31; financial
　transfer payment 84; information
　support 56, 111, 114–15;
　metropolitan area index 2; taxation 8

Tangshan 94–5, 102–4
taxes 29, 81
Tianjin 3, 8, 13, 18–19, 35, 67, 77–82,

84, 91, 94–5, 98, 100, 102–6, 109,
　111; government of 98, 100; local
　government of 95; part of the
　economic center of Northern China
　95; region 80–1
Tianjin-Hebei Metropolitan Area 101
*Tianjin's Promotion of Bohai Coastal
　Regional Cooperation* 98
Tokyo metropolitan area 6, 10
transfer payments 62, 81, 84, 113
transportation 3, 9, 12, 29, 58, 63, 86,
　95–6, 106, 115, 117; allocations for
　57; inconvenient 57; integration 16;
　and land planning 56
trust 14, 19–20, 39–40, 58, 61–5, 71,
　91, 105, 110, 112, 116; building of
　104, 111; and communication
　mechanism 8, 14, 19–20, 40, 45, 47,
　61–2, 104–5, 109–10; cooperative
　71; imperfect 93; relationships 62–3,
　71
tunnels 27

UCINET software 16, 91, 96, 100, 102
unemployed workers 81
urban agglomerations 6, 23, 34, 36, 38,
　41, 113; cooperation with compound
　administrations 36; governance
　structure 34; model 35
urban areas 2–3
urban functions 3, 35, 104
urbanization 2–3, 7, 11, 15, 34, 112

visual network of local government
　collaborations in the Beijing-
　Tianjin-Hebei metropolitan area
　from 2004 to 2007 *101*
visual network of local government
　collaborations in the Beijing-
　Tianjin-Hebei metropolitan area
　from 2008 to 2011 *101*

Wallis, Allan D. 24
waste 26, 74; incineration plants 26;
　solid 26, 74; treatment plants 73
water 9, 27, 70, 80–1, 84–5, 105–6;
　clean 74; consumption 80–1;
　domestic 8; emissions trading 85;
　environment security 8; governance
　75; pollution 8, 57, 67, 73, 76–7, 84,